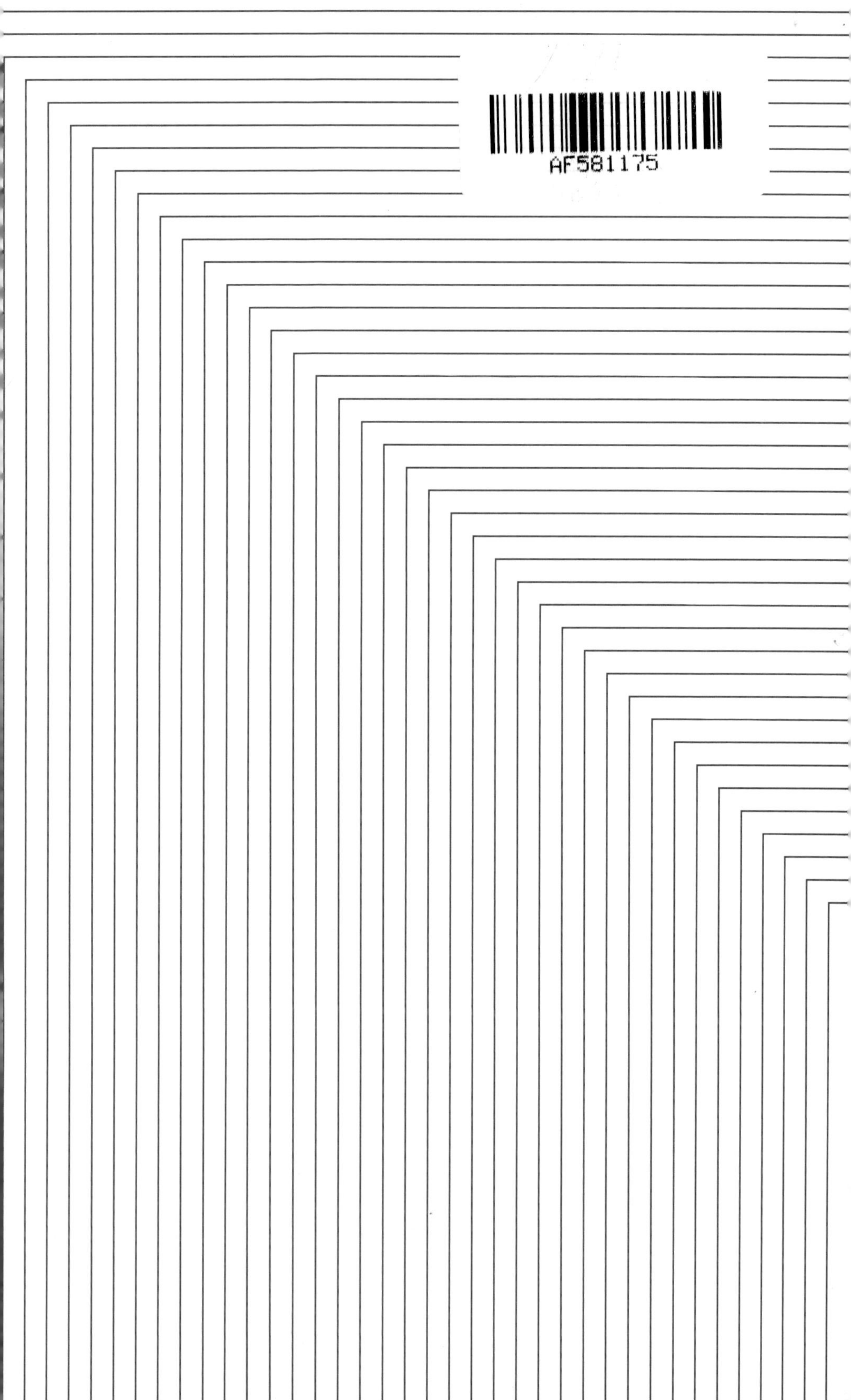
AF581175

The Pragmatism in the History of Art

Pre

INVENTORY PRESS

Occupations (1)

The PRAGMATISM in the HISTORY of ART

Molly Nesbit

Tuzenbakh: Life will remain the same as ever not just in two hundred or three hundred years but even in a million; life doesn't change, it remains constant, following its own particular laws, which don't concern you, or which at least you will never know. Migratory birds, cranes for example, fly and fly, and whatever thoughts, big or little, stray through their heads, they will still fly on without knowing why or where to. They fly and they will go on flying, whatever philosophers are born among them; and they can talk philosophy as much as they like, only they must fly on...

Masha: But what's the meaning of it?

Tuzenbakh: Meaning... Look, it's snowing. What meaning is there in that?

Anton Chekhov, *Three Sisters*

FIRST, a certain, involuntary pragmatism, which will linger like the corner of a shadow bending through the night. A pre-existence. A red cardinal's foregone song. It is windy. Someone comes with a time and a place. Initially that place was Berkeley.

William James put the philosophy of pragmatism forward during a lecture at the University of California in 1898. He avoided simplification and gloss. The new concept would be dense, enlightened and, before all else, modern. It had no single color. He drew closer, explaining to those present that "the effective meaning of any philosophic proposition can always be brought down to some particular consequence, in our future practical experience, whether active or passive; the point lying rather in the fact that the experience must be particular."[1]

The particular is to be known and will come to mean something because of a subsequent effect—something done perhaps, or something seen or heard or touched. Most important is its specificity, the close and restless focus, and although James does not say so exactly, its relation to a human scale. None of it stays small.

James credited his friend Charles Sanders Peirce with the concept pragmatism, though he himself was extending it. Elsewhere James would liken the theory to an instrument, not a picture, not an answer, and see the pragmatist to have an attitude that turns away from first things—principles, categories, supposed necessities—and instead trains the mind on last things—fruits, consequences, facts.[2] We could supply any number of examples—green strawberries, wars of religion, the temperature of the air at dawn. But the pragmatists brought their own catalysts. Thought would both appear and act as they moved it, relatively, into the details of a world they hoped to know better. In that, they were optimists.

Peirce, a man of completely singular mind, had drafted the first formulation of pragmatism twenty years earlier, in 1877, in a pair of articles, "The Fixation of Belief" and "How to Make Ideas Clear." Dry, stunning sentences set the new tone. "Nothing new," he had remarked, "can ever be learned by analyzing definitions."[3] All the same, it must be said that Peirce himself had begun by testing a definition, the *pragmatisch* in Kant, but he had jumped well past the philosophical terminology of the Germans by the time he penned the two articles, which would be published on both sides of the Atlantic in *Popular Science Monthly* and in the *Revue philosophique de la France et de l'étranger*. Ideas would achieve their clarity by virtue of producing habits of action, he told his readers, these being *effects* that were sensed and had practical bearing. He opened matters out into the nineteenth-century's own contribution to the experimental sciences; he made a point of testing his ideas, posing precisely physical problems for logic, for thought seen and run.

Peirce's examples still cut sharp; some shine; sometimes odd humor flickers over them; edges fall away. He set the hard against the soft, had diamonds disappear, untouched, into cotton; he introduced doubts creeping up into a mind that waited for a train; he let the waiting mind open wide, images accelerating so rapidly through it that they melted before the train could come. He saw reality ultimately to be independent of an individual person's thoughts.

How to know? Peirce had no problem breaking pace to quote an entire stanza from Thomas Gray's "Elegy Written in a Country Churchyard." Under these conditions, logic, scientific advance, danger and art would not condense into a new compound or unified field theory; instead each would contribute in its own way to reveal different aspects of life, even those that man himself might never see:

Full many a gem of purest ray serene
    The dark unfathom'd caves of ocean bear:
Full many a flower is born to blush unseen,
    And waste its sweetness on the desert air.[4]

Such was the ideal that James decided to hold aloft in 1898. After his lectures, for there were many, a momentum built internationally for the pragmatism coming from America. Peirce too added more. Peirce refined his sense of what a pragmatist could do; he set to work on language and logic. He and James were not always in perfect synch. For one thing, Peirce would not want to give up on the use of generality; in his later work he came to stress the importance of continuity. Yet Peirce, like James, wanted the pragmatist to ask the largest possible questions about the place of all of this and us in time. Some of this ambition is present in statements like: "The rational meaning of every proposition lies in the future."[5] Or: "You need not fear to compromise your darling theory by looking out at its windows."[6] He expected the pragmatist to look outside to weigh the world. The particular consequence? The future of man.

The future overtook them both. Peirce died in 1914, James in 1910, but by then John Dewey had joined the effort and himself done much to secure the global stage for these ideas. He extended them in other directions. Dewey went far beyond the window sashes, put pragmatism together with social reform and gave this thinking other kinds of practical traction. He was becoming the great American philosopher of education. He felt it important to turn knowledge toward the creation of a dynamic, responsible and democratic public consciousness. He wrote of living *forward*.

In early 1917, while most of Europe had gone to war and the United States continued to wait, Dewey was still hoping to maintain his own pacifism and full freedom of speech. It was then that he gave the questions a general, and unprotected, place to stand. Henceforth they would be posted there, subject to whatever rode in. "Knowing," he announced, "is viewing from the outside." It was no longer conceivable to stay near the windows or contemplate slim ivoried towers. The problems of the day required more—a different understanding of where knowledge exists and how it grows. The significant distinctions are to be made, Dewey wrote, "between the different ways of being in and of the movement of things; between a brute physical way and a purposive, intelligent way."[7] The United States entered World War I in April 1917. The war ended with the armistice in November 1918. In 1919, in protest against Columbia University's censure of its antiwar faculty, Dewey gave his support to the group that founded the New School for Social Research. He took a leave from Columbia for two years to teach in Japan and China.

In 1925, at the end of his book *Experience and Nature,* Dewey would give art a key role to play. By then he had spent years traveling abroad, lecturing and listening. When Chinese students rioted in Beijing in 1919 and the May 4th movement broke out, he was, as it happened, there. His speeches and books remained enormously influential, and his own sense of how to put thought forward was constantly being tested in new situations. Dewey saw art to be both a tool and a fundamental form of practice in service of the gargantuan, ephemeral experiment that is life. All art had and would continue to have a use—it brought an education to perception, new modes of perception; it became the means to future sight. For Dewey, the new modern art was neither an alien nor an abstraction taken on faith; it too had the capacity to act as a catalyst. Experience in the form of art, he called it, and saw it as a way to bring mind and matter together "so that he who runs may read," exhibiting the fact "that consciousness is not a separate realm of being, but is the manifest quality of existence when nature is most free and most active."[8]

Dewey lectured in Mexico in 1926. The Soviets invited him to tour their still unfinished state and to speak on education in the summer of 1928. Soviet political theory did not impress him much, but Dewey appreciated the contact with the Russian people, their will and their new world in the making. He watched the Western economies reel as the stock markets crashed the next year and the idea of fearless growth was caught short. He saw new orders moving into place, not always rationally. He learned. He kept thinking. Art was not arriving as an afterthought to pragmatism; it was spawning more. In 1934 Dewey published *Art as Experience*, the book that made these ideas clear. It was dedicated to William James.[9] In its preface he thanked the young art historian Meyer Schapiro for his help.

Now more than three-quarters of a century later, we walk in their future. Yet their pragmatism does not in and of itself explain or become our script. There is no script. The pragmatism of Peirce and James and Dewey exists as it moved, absorbing and absorbed. The strawberries remain green, the wars of religion are ongoing, the air at dawn is freezing. *La chaîne est belle* but scarce foretold. Conclusions remain provisions, time riding on, perpetually unsettled, nocturnal, opaque. Many questions and conditions remain. They will recur. The future has not eased. In our own lifetime there have been stakes, some old, some new, in continuing to write about the time and place and point of art. It is important to mark them. Pragmatism is above all a way of working, it starts from the present. That said, no one works unmoored, or alone.

Paris

When Michel Foucault died in the spring of 1984, his friend and fellow philosopher Gilles Deleuze began a book that he would call, simply, *Foucault,* and lift the great problem of the "death of man" back into Foucault's thought as something still alive, something that had altered both things and knowledge too. Foucault had left a *pensée* possessed of breadth and a clarity as it plunged through things that were political, literary, and metaphysical in nature. Toward the end of his *Foucault,* Deleuze drew this picture of the depths.

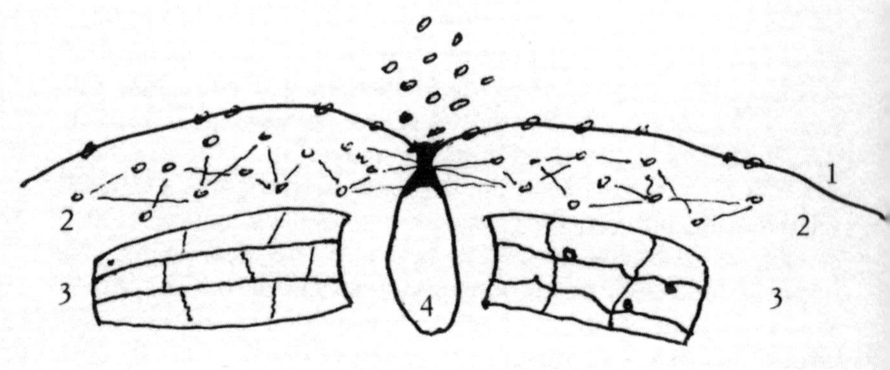

Gilles Deleuze, Diagram of the Thought of Michel Foucault, *Foucault* (Paris: Minuit, 1986) p. 128.

Every now and then Deleuze would remark upon Foucault's pragmatism.[10] By that he meant a process and a method that had posed a series of questions for knowledge. Deleuze had in mind Foucault's *Discipline and Punish,* a *summa* where the process of seeing collided so violently with the question of visibility that perception itself, judgment too, broke apart and went specific. Invisible barriers and channels were revealed to be shaping, and continuing to shape, the ordained picture of modern life. *Discipline and Punish* spent pages detailing the operation of the panopticon where, from a central tower, the entire business of the prison could be monitored without any need for patrol. Foucault described it as a laboratory of power. In the early nineteenth century the panopticon would give its model over to other bodies seeking to centralize dominion—governments, factories, hospitals and schools.[11] But the example of the panopticon was but one among many points, some steely, some scorching, some barely limned, from which Foucault composed his philosophical paths. Deleuze spoke to the pragmatism that became books like *Discipline and Punish* and pointed to the tracks that had been covered, like the manuscript on Manet, which Foucault had quietly destroyed.[12]

Some of these routes were Nietzschean. Deleuze did not mention the period when he and Foucault had worked together on a French edition of Nietzsche; he spoke instead of the ways Nietzsche had marked his friend's thought. In many ways the problems undertaken by Nietzsche had much in common with those being examined during the same years by Peirce: for one thing, the problem of science itself, which Nietzsche had seen as knowledge-altering and altogether new. Nietzsche hoped initially, he later reflected, to view science from the perspective of the artist, and to look at art in the perspective of life.[13] This led him to try to forge a Philosophy of the Future, "*a critique of modernity*, not excluding modern sciences, modern arts and even modern politics."[14]

Foucault's pragmatism too had been born from mulling over Kant's *pragmatisch*, from there to fix on the separation that took Kant off into the unsteady school of the world, meaning by that an order of knowledge distinct from that pursued in Kant's *Critiques*, an order closer to the one Goethe described in *Wilhelm Meister*, his great *Bildungsroman*.[15] In the early 1960s Foucault undertook to see the pragmatic part of Kant's thought philologically, part of an historical process of thought that would tie philosophy to the questions about man being asked in the German sciences. He invoked Nietzsche's *Ubermensch* as he signed off; like Nietzsche, he pronounced another *Morgenrot*, a Daybreak. Even in his early work, Foucault was determined to jump ahead. He would make the question of man temporal. He would also make it temporary.

All this would help Foucault set the problem of knowledge's ruptures and mutations for *The Order of Things*, the book that would give him an international reputation when it was published in 1966.[16] He became especially interested in the empirical and nonformal procedures through which knowledge might be gained. When he wrote the preface to the English-language edition in 1970, he put these matters up front. "This foreword should perhaps be headed 'Directions for Use'," he informed his public.[17] Further on in the preface he posted an injunction: "I should like this work to be read as an open site. Many questions are laid out on it that have not yet found answers; and many of the gaps refer either to earlier works or to others that have not yet been completed, or even begun."[18]

Discipline and Punish became his next long book. It laid out its objects in case histories that marked out a territory for the questions raised: philosophy proceeded accordingly, not always logically; the particulars sometimes harbored the most traditional of abstract questions and worked them open like clay. Via the history of legality, the order of things was being analyzed in a literal way as a matter of life and death, crime and punishment, production and education. Foucault worked with techniques lifted from the different drawers and compartments of knowledge: he weighed the treatises against the codes, and against the accounts of witnesses and the ongoing analyses of scientists, all of them fragments inflecting and sometimes structuring the procedures and practices of law and social judgment. He documented some sources and let others speak at length, quoted and credited, inside his own arguments. He let the empirical material keep its shell, respected its intractibility and strange allure. He knew that writing, even in hindsight, could not produce complete transparency. He was writing about the past, but made it clear that his subject extended into and existed, still alive and beating, still largely masked, in the present.[19] It was 1975.

What characterizes Foucault's pragmatism, and this would also be true of Deleuze's work at the time, is its insistence upon particular ideas, a singular case, a lone thing unremarked, an isolated effect and its capacity, for better or worse, to change, dissociate, move. Use will have directions too: such a philosophy-in-progress grows outward from decidedly historical material, from a ground, and it is meant to have a general, even public application. This is why Deleuze underscored Foucault's own distinction between the historical research he, as a philosopher, had undertaken and the finished, often insular work of the professional historian.[20] Foucault in his late work framed the matter variously but often cited a minor article Kant had written for a newspaper in 1784. The newspaper had posed Kant the question "What is the Enlightenment [*Aufklärung*]?"

Kant had placed this question in his own, late eighteenth-century present, the one we now call the dawn of the modern. He would eventually give it company–a second question, "What brings about the will to revolution?" For Foucault, this sideline in Kant provoked a different kind of thinking with historical material. Foucault considered the question "*Qu'est-ce que c'est que notre actualité?*" "What is our actuality?" and "What then is the actual field of possible experiences?" to be founding questions for philosophy, ones that asked to be taken specifically—but not in service to the analytic of truth, the philosophical tradition most associated with Kant. Foucault wanted to carry these questions toward an ontology of the rough present.[21] Such questions about enlightenment and actuality would not suddenly strip the philosopher of his abstract abilities, or high mountains. These words merely asked that the philosopher cross paths beyond his discipline, speak and break camp with others, like historians, for example, and then head out. On the paths the historian could find some common cause as well with the renegade. There were good prospects. None of this alone would actually *answer* the questions. The open site lay waiting, destined to be wide.

In 1972 Deleuze and Foucault put together a conversation in which this pragmatism found another footing. They used it to develop a politics but not only that: "A theory," Deleuze said to Foucault, "is exactly like a box of tools. It has nothing to do with the signifier. It must be useful. It must function. And not for itself. If no one uses it, beginning with the theoretician himself (who then ceases to be a theoretician), then the theory is worthless or the moment is inappropriate. We don't revise a theory, but construct new ones; we have no choice but to make others." He then held up a tool, so to speak, continuing the thought as he did so: "It is strange that it was Proust, an author thought to be a pure intellectual, who said it so clearly: treat my book as a pair of glasses directed to the outside; if they don't suit you, find another pair; I leave it to you to find your own instrument, which is necessarily an investment for combat."[22] The conversation and its tropes have been a touchstone ever since. The two were exhibiting a pragmatism that explicitly invites several voices at once to co-exist in discussions that were actual and ready to be inherited; this was not to be a philosophy of the monologue. It, too, was a philosophy of the future.

Deleuze would sum up Foucault's entire philosophy as "*une pragmatique du multiple*"; at the same time he would underscore Foucault's persistent attempts to chart what in English would be called "the outside."[23] Perhaps he put it best in the diagram. It seems to derive from a page drawn by one of their favorite artists, Paul Klee. Klee, as part of his teaching at the Bauhaus in the twenties, had been concerned with assembling the toolbox for modern art. He had begun, like most of his peers, with geometries and looked through them to construct hybrid lesson plans for young artists.[24] He unleashed the straight line so that it might run past the boundaries of precedent; he let the line act out a seed's germination, the pollination of a fruit blossom and the physiology of a heart. Deleuze's diagram was much less idyllic: it exposed the active thought of the philosopher mole, the one waiting impatiently for daybreak.

Deleuze drew Foucault's thought folded underground, neither solid nor void, sunk but not interred in a school of the earth, working on seeing and saying and yet conscious of the physical forces all around; thought is being released into them. He invoked completely extraneous examples, triggers really, from American literature: there was Herman Melville following the fissure and fearing a vast void at the end; there was William Faulkner describing a struggle so

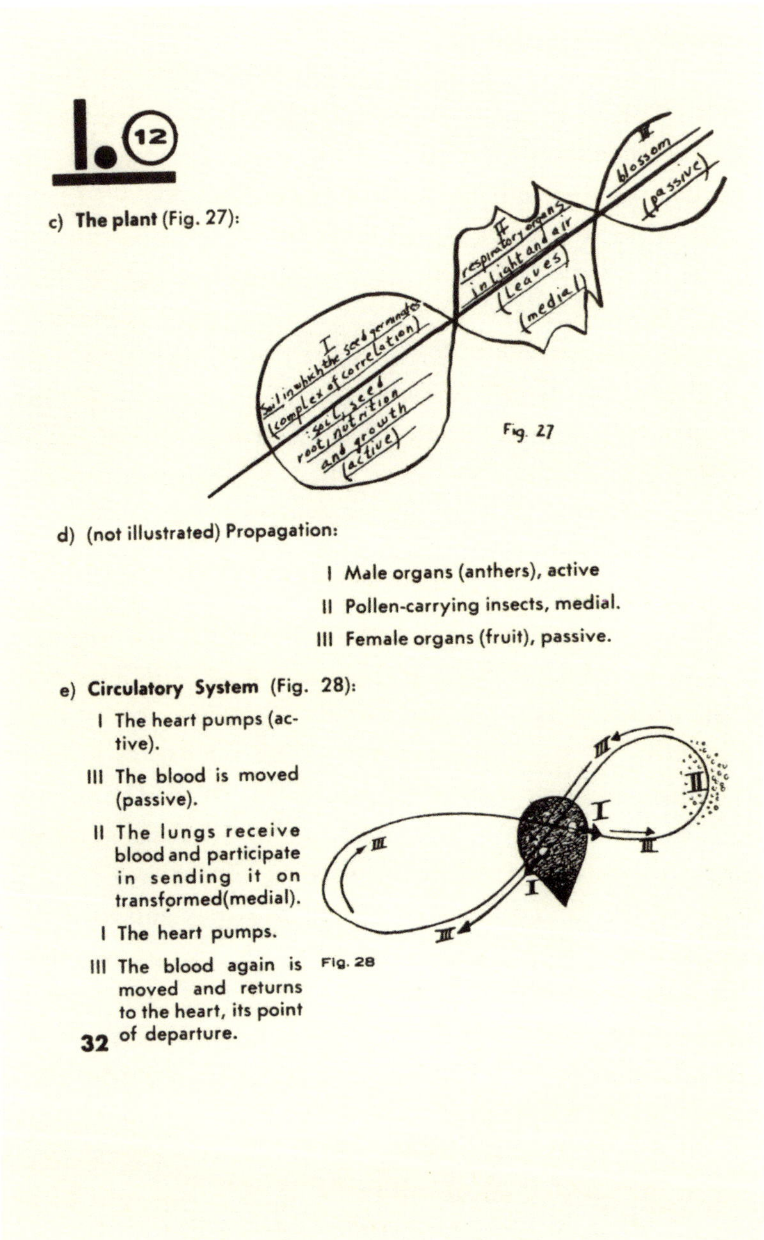

I.12

c) **The plant** (Fig. 27):

d) (not illustrated) Propagation:

I Male organs (anthers), active

II Pollen-carrying insects, medial.

III Female organs (fruit), passive.

e) **Circulatory System** (Fig. 28):

I The heart pumps (active).

III The blood is moved (passive).

II The lungs receive blood and participate in sending it on transformed (medial).

I The heart pumps.

III The blood again is moved and returns to the heart, its point of departure.

32

Paul Klee, *Pedagogical Sketchbook*, 1925 (London: Faber & Faber, 1953) p. 32.

all-consuming that people became more like moths or feathers rising above a hurricane as they raged on to the death.[25] This is an outside premised on storm, strong images, sublimity and force. But the diagram charts a dynamic of stress and equilibrium. Down in the fold, thought navigates the gusts, like a boat heading out, sailing, not sinking.

There can be no end to such a thought's odyssey, its quest for effect. The same intrepid attitude, call it pragmatic, Deleuze did, marks the book he and Félix Guattari put out in 1980, *A Thousand Plateaus*. It would become the *Thousand and One Nights* for the next generation's dream of freedom. But the plateaus, though loaded with examples even wilder and more iridescent than those of Peirce, their hero, were grounded. Pragmatics, Deleuze and Guattari claimed, is the fundamental element on which logic, syntax and semantics depend; and it is pragmatism that becomes a *politics* of language.[26] Or, Deleuze would write later in an essay on Herman Melville's "Bartleby," pragmatism is the double-principle of archipelago and hope launching untold perspectives.

By then it was 1989 and Deleuze was bringing this pragmatism to bear on the old Cold Warriors. He yoked their history together. The United States had come forward with its pragmatism, he explained; the Soviets had brought their dialectic. In his estimation, both their revolutions, their bids for the future, had failed. The surviving pragmatist was not playing the role of the proverbial businessman; the present world was but a wall of loose stones. Yet pragmatism, Deleuze maintained, was not well understood if limited to being an older American school of philosophy. It was still a project whose *fragments* were being mobilized in quest of truth and trust. It might seem noble, deserving the best of all possible destinies, but Deleuze did not forecast a happy end. The pragmatists he cited were not Peirce, James or Dewey; his pragmatists were Bartleby, and Henry James' Daisy Miller and Melville's Pierre and Isabelle, all of them nineteenth-century fictions with original, unbending souls that in the end were thwarted.[27] What then? And the world of the future?

If the forces are historical, and matter is indeed material, the trade in pragmatism described so far cannot be sewn up at this point, made eternal for the twenty-first century, or trimmed like a sail. It was and is by nature an actual exchange and as such it should be understood as an ongoing effect of the Americans and the French having fought two World Wars together in the twentieth century and then needing to fathom the reasons why. The ensuing pragmatism bespeaks that long and rich and vexed situation. It sprang from waves of death. On the positive side, it returned everyone to agreed-upon starting points for the definition of modernity, first to the French and American Revolutions and the eighteenth-century's Enlightenment, then to the nineteenth-century city, specifically to the triumph of capital both damned and celebrated in Paris. It was not forgotten that each starting point came soaked in political violence. But there were other, unexpected starting points contributing pulse.

In the 1930s the attention of the French reading public had turned to the latest American literature being translated and promoted by André Malraux, Valéry Larbaud and Jean-Paul Sartre. In the summer of 1939, just before the Nazis invaded Poland, Sartre praised *The Sound and the Fury* to the skies. In Faulkner's tale Sartre saw the present chasing another present away, over and over again, adding up to make a line that could only be rendered by breaks: <<and...and...and then>>. They were adding up holes, holes in time.[28]

They made their mark on French film a generation later. While at *lycée,* in Neuilly, at the western edge of Paris, in 1938, Chris Marker had been at student in Sartre's philosophy class and Sartre was telling them too about the breakthroughs in American novels. He gave them an essay to publish in the literary magazine Marker and his friends were calling *Le trait d'union,* union's trait being as well the French for hyphen. Sartre's essay, which was on Dos Passos, began the idea that would be taken up the next year when he wrote about Faulkner. He introduced Dos Passos as a storyteller able to create his own order of time, a memory savoring the present, where memories were tied–to facts:

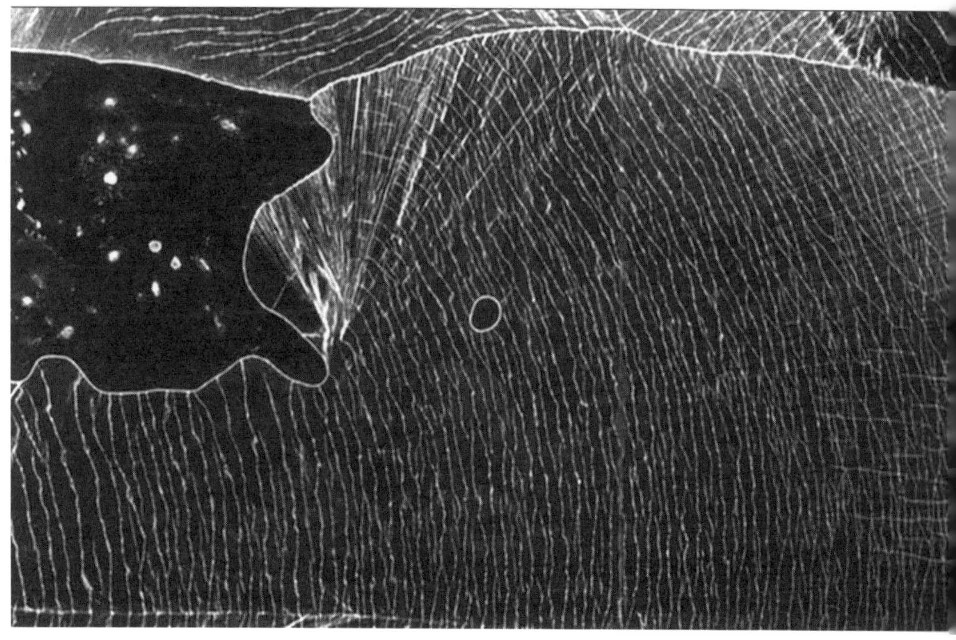

Chris Marker, Still from *La Jetée*, 1962.

> Each event is irreducible, a gleaming and solitary *thing* that does not flow from anything else, but suddenly arises to join other things. For Dos Passos, narrating means adding. This accounts for the slack air of his style. <<And...and...and...>>. The great disturbing phenomena—war, love, political movements, strikes—fade and crumble into an infinity of little odds and ends which can just about be set side by side.[29]

Was it by accident that the next July time would break into the addition and his idea, scattering the ends and odds? Sartre ended his essay on Faulkner insisting on the hopes, possibilities and the necessity of holding out the future. Even in a time paralyzed, suffocating, dying of its own old age, where the only option looked like cataclysm, the one we now call World War II.

Much later, in 1962, Chris Marker made the film *La Jetée*, set just after a future World War III. It was the story of a man marked by an image of his childhood. As for the story itself, Marker later said that it had come in from outside, like automatic writing. "It just happened, that's all," he observed. "I photographed a story I hardly understood." Adding, "it's in the cutting room that the pieces of the puzzle came together, and it wasn't me who designed the puzzle."[30] As if an odyssey ripe with fate had pulled the pieces to the jetty, pieces born from the delta of too many experiences, those read, those felt from his own time at war, in labor camp, in the *maquis,* in Asia and in the American National Exhibition in Moscow in the summer of 1959, where he had marveled at the gigantic seven-screen slide show projection, *Glimpses of the U. S. A.,* by Charles and Ray Eames. There, in Moscow, in a twelve-minute rhythm all its own, was an American workday coupled with an American weekend day, stills interrupted once by a film clip of Marilyn Monroe taken from the *Seven Year Itch.* Marker had carried the book of a day, Joyce's *Ulysses,* with him as he went off into the *maquis.*[31] Once down in the delta, experience sheds its cause.

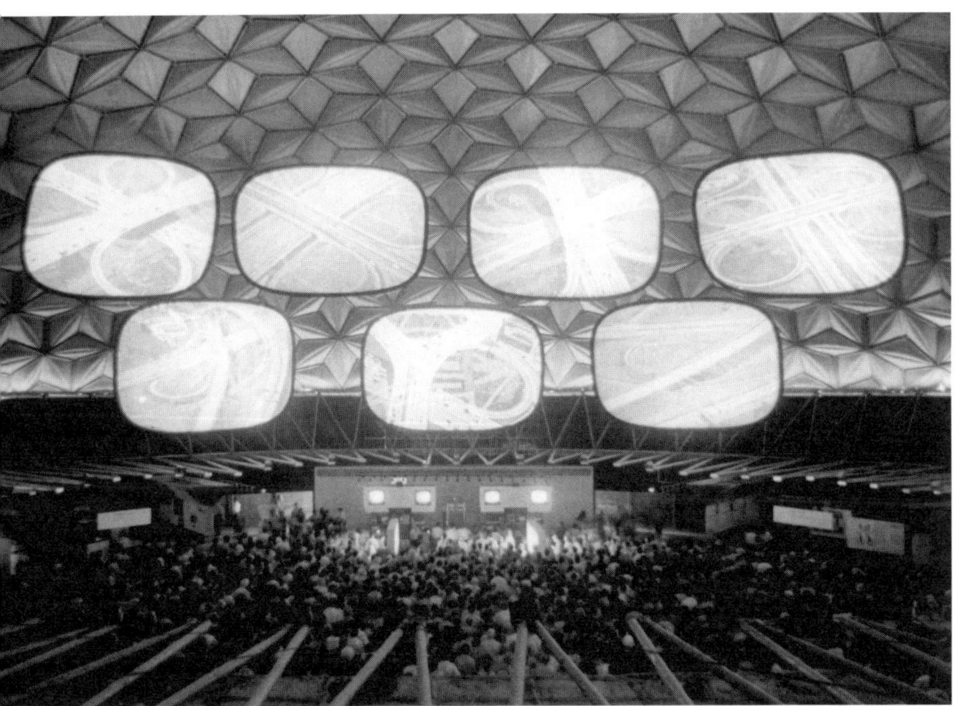

Charles and Ray Eames, *Glimpses of the U. S. A.,* 1959. Seven-screen projection for the American National Exhibition in Moscow, 1959.

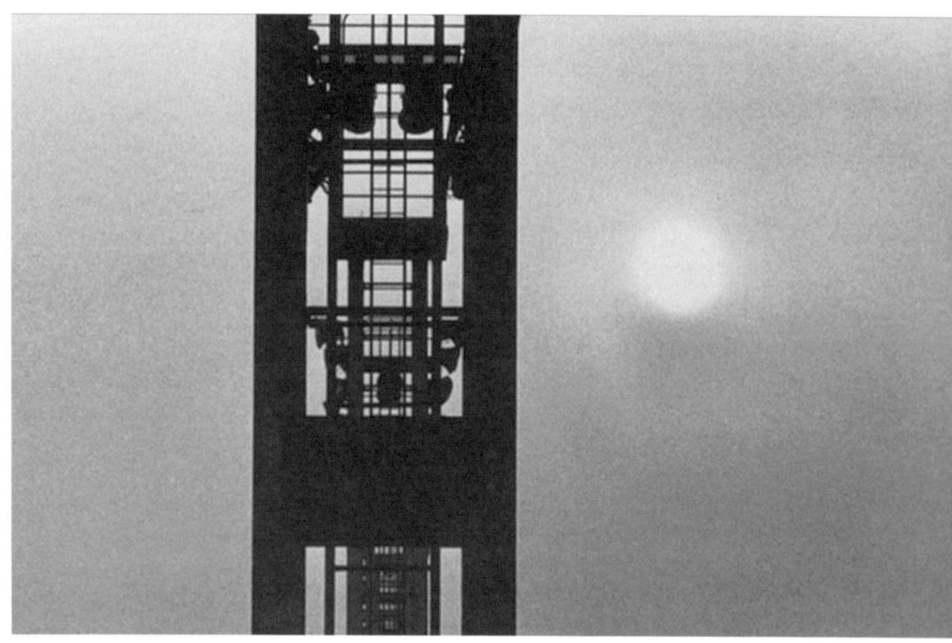

Chris Marker, Still from *La Jetée*, 1962.

La Jetée began on a jetty at Orly on a Sunday, with a frozen sun and a tempo that moved a plot backward and forward through the holes in time, time opened and closed by isolated, still images, burn and echo, images so powerful that they propelled an entire film along, a succession of stops and turns, the cuts between them felt more and more deeply as the film went on. At one point, and only one, the image moved and then seized up again. The image held the doors to life and time, it seemed, if it could be opened. The most potent of them all showed a single woman's face. A hole in time can be held in a photograph. Day can turn to night, and death, the hole in life.

Ten years later, in the early 1970s, Jean-Luc Godard built a montage around the ‹‹and›› as he and his Dziga Vertov collective tried to communicate the substance of the fedayeen's struggle to win back Palestine. Their video came to be called *Here and Elsewhere*. Deleuze would underscore the staggered movement of this ‹‹and›› when he wrote about Godard's video work a few years later, in 1976. The two of them had been talking. The idea eventually took Deleuze to a meditation where ‹‹and›› ceded to *between*. The *between*

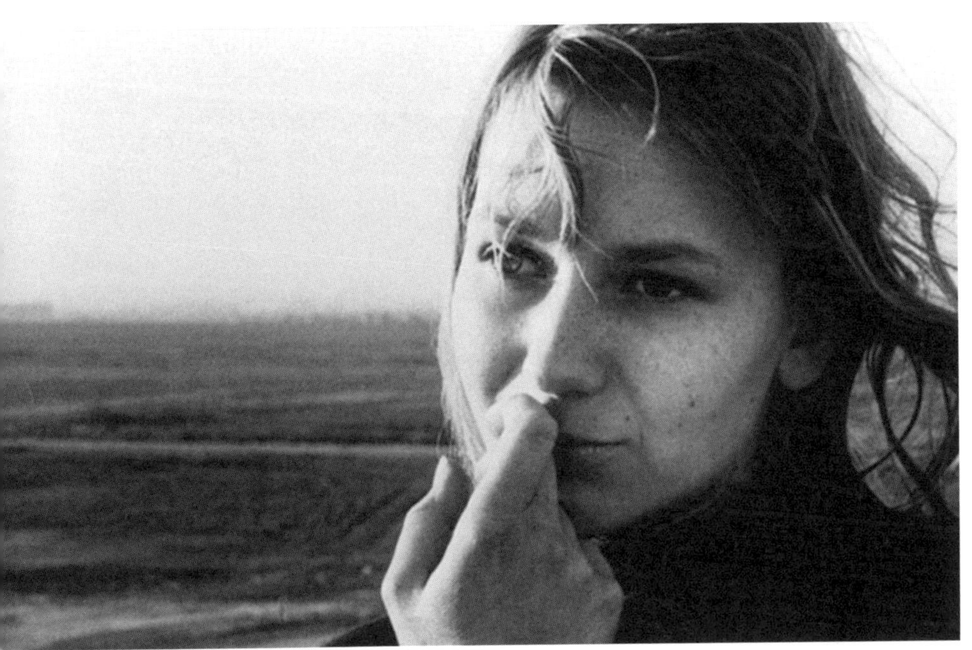

Chris Marker, Still from *La Jetée*, 1962.

that would not only open the *Thousand Plateaus,* it would plunge and plough:

> It is American, and even earlier, English literature that have shown this rhizomatic direction, have known how to insinuate themselves between things, to install a logic of AND, overturn ontology, impoverish the foundation, annul ends and starts. They have known how to make a pragmatics. The middle is not at all an average, it is, on the contrary, the place where things pick up speed. *Between* things does not designate a locatable relation which goes from one to the other, and reciprocally so, but rather a perpendicular direction, a transversal movement that carries them–one *and* the other, stream without beginning or end–gnaws at both banks and takes on speed in the middle.[32]

Pragmatism being known through a line of examples, one pragmatism chases another pragmatism away. They leave their trace now as so many scenes. Pure presents keep ceding. People come and go. Earth rises and falls. Hearts beat. Words pass. It falls to history to study the nature of change and to chase the present's trail into time's grey ebb. It may take a while to realize that history is nothing less than an eternal, punishing hunt for the present—no matter when it happened.

The present is not a simple object beating a retreat; it can also strike like a thief, unbidden, from without. Peirce caught its glint when he recited Gray. The director Mike Nichols captured something of it when he noted in passing that for first-rate artists, at some point early on, "`the time`" just flows into them, once and only once; he said it came without any planning.[33] And after the breach? What happens to "`the time`"? It is not to be summarized as an idea. Those who have felt it will never call it an ideal. It can happen that a present goes forward long-term, even longer than a lifetime; it can happen to be short. Sometimes a work of art can hold it.

How to catch a present? Write it down? No writing, not even history, is stable. The current catches everything. One art history will chase another art history away. For the matters to hand, this will require a separate discussion now, one with its own modernity. This again will be a French and American tale, at least in part. It is not unrelated to the one already being told.

New York

The writing of modern art history is dated to the 1930s. It is often tied to the essays of the young Meyer Schapiro, in particular his review of the exhibition *Cubism and Abstract Art,* the international survey of avant-garde art organized in the spring of 1936 by Alfred Barr Jr. at the new Museum of Modern Art. Barr had given modern art its own line of evolution, one that pushed all the avant-gardes together into one encompassing movement, as if it were a species in full-blown evolution, everything inclined toward an end state of either "geometric" or "non-geometric" abstraction. One single category was being brought in to do the job of gathering an ungainly whole into a destiny. Only formal values embodied in compositions of color, line, light and shade were recognized as identifiers, or worthwhile. Never mind the undergrowth. Paul Klee might have been working to expand the semiotic heft of his lines but Barr's exhibition emphasized radical contraction. *Cubism and Abstract Art* installed a strict formalism based on an aesthetics of separation—from religion, from politics, from anything recognizable in the outer world.[34] Nothing in art could be binding. No image was allowed to hold open a door to time. Real futures, just like the actual present, were to be kept away.

In his review, Schapiro, who was teaching at Columbia University and at the New School for Social Research, refuted Barr's rather too elegant proposition outright.[35] He had another view altogether of modern art. Before the show even opened, Schapiro delivered a talk at the New School to the American Artists' Congress on "The Social Bases of Art." He spoke at some length about the different schools of modern artists. He saw each to have its own characteristic objects deriving from "a context of experience" lodged as well in their individual, chosen forms.[36] None of it was simple. Modern artists had been wrestling with the social origins of their forms and experience alike, he noted, origins that privileged the consumption and enjoyment of elites, origins that had relegated the public to the margins. His was a large, and avowedly Marxist, argument against aesthetic separation. And if not separated? Not

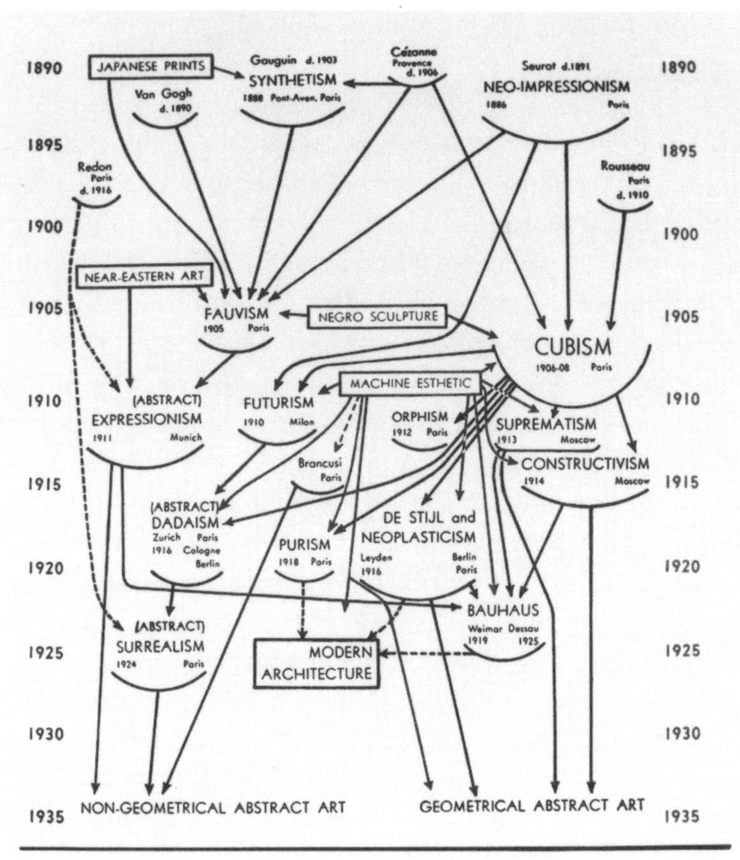

Alfred Barr Jr., Chart on the Dust Jacket of *Cubism and Abstract Art* (New York: The Museum of Modern Art, 1936).

alienated? Much would have to change. "An individual art in a society where human beings do not feel themselves to be most individual when they are inert, dreaming, passive, tormented, or uncontrolled would be very different from modern art," he wrote. "And in a society where all men can be free individuals, individuality must lose its exclusiveness and its ruthless and perverse character."[37] Such were the contradictions that lay before the individual, artist or not.

His critique of *Cubism and Abstract Art* was published in the January 1937 issue of *Marxist Quarterly*, a new academic journal where he was the art editor. The review would begin from the premises of "The Social Bases" and involve a sustained consideration of the "Nature of Abstract Art," the title he decided to use. He explained more fully the perspectives he saw holding the work of the individual artist in their grip and then he doubled back on them, declaring, "there is no 'pure art' unconditioned by experience; all fantasy and formal construction, even the random scribbling of the hand, are shaped by experience and by non-esthetic concerns."[38] He described the experimental nature of those working out the new abstractions.[39] He argued that the variety in abstraction spoke out against any attempt to condense it into a strictly internal, aesthetic logic: "it bears within itself at almost every point the mark of the changing material and psychological conditions surrounding modern culture."[40] This would put another valuation on nature. He saw the philosophy of art to be a philosophy of life and said so.

In the early twentieth century it was no secret that abstract art was developing in relation to industrialization. Schapiro proposed that the relation between the two be seen anew and plainly, not as a mirror reflection but as an interplay of escalating implication. There was no consensus as to what the abstract forms would themselves express. There were surprises. He pointed out that the most advanced industrial countries, the United States and Britain, were not the points of origin for the new mechanical abstractions. Instead it was Italy, Holland, Germany and the Soviet Union that had witnessed the creation of distinct abstractions that were each putting forward their own local conditions and social conflicts. The older categories of art were being translated, variously, into what Schapiro termed "the language of modern technology" where "the essential was identified with the efficient, the unit with the standardized element, texture with new materials, representation with photography, drawing with the ruled or mechanically traced line, color with the flat coat of paint, and design with the model or instructing plan."[41] The artists had joined their labor, aesthetically, to the abstract calculations of the engineer and the scientist, as equal partners. And then the Great Depression had come in the 1930s and reset those trajectories. Since then, Schapiro thought, the mechanically based styles had lost their inevitability and cultural force. Surrealism was rising to greater prominence. His appraisal of the nature of abstract art stopped on that point, before revolution.

Schapiro had picked up tools from Dewey's *Art as Experience* to shape his critique. Dewey had also concluded with a meditation on the industrial conditions of civilization as a whole. He had noted that they were producing new ways of seeing, new habits of the human eye, which for him was the crucial medium for perception. "The colors and planes to which the organism habitually responds develop new material for interest," he wrote. "The running brook, the greensward, the forms associated with a rural environment, are losing their place as the primary material of experience."[42] The values that came with the mechanical modes of production were saturating the old landscape; they were promoting aesthetic change too but could they produce the former satisfactions, given the labor problems, the injustices that accompanied the change? The machine aesthetics were not going to be his problem. Dewey's book ended elsewhere:

> What is true is that art itself is not secure under modern conditions until the mass of men and women who do the useful work of the world have the opportunity to be free in conducting the processes of production and are richly endowed in capacity for enjoying the fruits of collective work. That the material for art should be drawn from all sources whatever and that the products of art should be accessible to all is a demand by the side of which the personal political intent of the artist is insignificant.[43]

The individual artist's politics could and should be subsumed into the greater, progressive social forces mobilizing for equality. He was their advocate.

Though Schapiro's own politics went more Marxist than Dewey's ever would, the givens in Dewey's view of art were assumptions taken into the vein and movement of Schapiro's thought at such a fundamental level that they did not need citation. Some of this was due to having taken class with Dewey in the twenties.[44] Only later, after Dewey's death, would Schapiro devote a long footnote to making the link public, explaining that Dewey's great insights bore on the "situations, problems, difficulties, obscure relationships of art and experience of art among other fields of our activity," the creative act, which artists themselves knew to be something unpredictable and mysterious. Schapiro called this an everyday creative activity, one "in which people work through difficulties, experiment, observe, change, destroy, start again, and finally bring their work to a conclusion, which is only the starting point of something new." Dewey's very ideas, he reflected, continue to remind us of the art of our own time and give Dewey the philosopher a place beside the great artists who have shaped the modern vision of life.[45]

There were so many ideas on Dewey's palette. In the early thirties, Dewey's public arguments against an aesthetics of separation led to the understanding of art as an experience writ long and large, and ordinary and raw. He understood art to be part of human existence in the social world and in the cosmos; it was a means of connection to mysteries that could only be approached. Dewey would use philosophy and scientific means, particularly psychology, to set and work these questions; he allowed artists to speak for their work unchallenged—Van Gogh, Cézanne, the British poets, Tolstoy; he listened as he wrote. He took against the kind of criticism that would measure art by a single standard—be it economic, political, psychoanalytic, sociological, religious or scientific; he upbraided T. S. Eliot for confusing aesthetic values with philosophical ones. It was the medium, Dewey argued, that made it possible for art to link the live being with his surroundings and produce the deepest vibration of experience.[46] The arguments he made did not much involve the analysis of particular forms, or pictures, though he emphasized that it was through the achieved work of art that the full interaction, the

Kasimir Malevich, *Painterly Realism of a Boy with Knapsack-Color Masses in the Fourth Dimension*, 1915. The Museum of Modern Art, New York.

existential perception, took place. As it happened, that attention to particular works of art would be Schapiro's contribution to pragmatism. Schapiro himself would have described it as a contribution to art history.

At one point in his review of Barr's exhibition, Schapiro broke from the category questions to consider a set of paintings by Kasimir Malevich. Barr had included *Painterly Realism of a Boy with Knapsack—Color Masses in the Fourth Dimension*, which at the time went by a simpler English title, *Suprematist Composition*. Schapiro wondered why Barr had failed to see that the balance of the squares had developed from an earlier painting Malevich had made of a peasant woman carrying two water pails. He then introduced a third painting, a still earlier one by Picasso where the problem of balance is posed by an acrobat, a circus child, alighting on a ball.[47] Balancing acts were not abstractions purely. Even the most geometric of works held the reference to the experience of the real world. Pails and balls weighed. Abstraction contained the memory of such intensive experience, of gravity; it could act as the conduit for extensive experiences too, for the forces that were sharply and irrevocably organizing modernity.

Later in 1937 Schapiro drafted an essay tentatively titled "The Arts Under Socialism"; it pondered the new techniques in architecture and painting and imagined their role in a classless society. It was probably written with the readership of the *Marxist Quarterly* in mind. The most radical styles would continue to develop, Schapiro thought, but they would be accompanied by the gradual disappearance of both painting and architecture: painting would withdraw and become private; architecture would become pure engineering. Painting on the whole would be transformed into film and the role the painter had performed heretofore would give way to that of the cinema director. In the finished product there would be no direct physical trace of the artist left since the film is reproduced mechanically and a team of people is required. Yet another advance would be forthcoming: "the form of the film is even more abstract than that of painting; for it is motion of various kinds; the most intangible metaphysical entity–the younger brother of space."[48]

Schapiro was far from alone in these observations. Gertrude Stein, who had once been a student of William James, said as much about the work of her friend Picasso. In 1938 she cast Picasso's paintings into a much larger consideration of the changes around all people in the twentieth century, changes that forced out what she decided to call the composition of a generation, by which she meant the way people, not paintings, live and see in the physical world. The picture had left its frame; life did not need the old frames.[49] The lack of stability, she

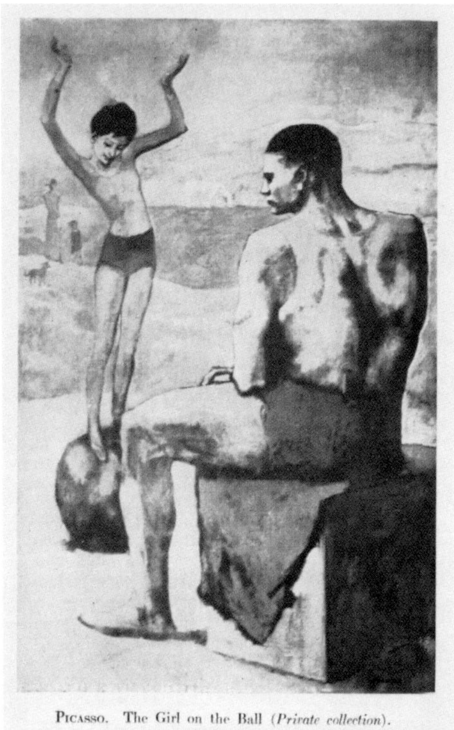

PICASSO. The Girl on the Ball (*Private collection*).

Pablo Picasso, *Acrobat on a Ball*, 1905, as it appeared in Eli Faure, *History of Art*, v. IV-Modern Art (New York: Harper & Brothers, 1924) p. 481.

went on to say, made for a change in the twentieth century with which one was simply obliged to live: "...as the twentieth century is a century which sees the earth as no one has ever seen it, the earth has a splendor that it never has had, and as everything destroys itself in the twentieth century and nothing continues, so then the twentieth century has a splendor which is its own and Picasso is of this century, he has that strange quality of an earth that one has never seen and of things destroyed as they have never been destroyed."[50]

Being crossed himself by historical forces, himself feeling the world shift abruptly around him, Schapiro wrote essays primarily. They let him keep pace. He chose topics that would enable him to contribute to the aesthetic issues he felt most pressing for Marxists. At one juncture he made of list of them:

I. Critique of the basic concepts used today in the investigation of art
   a. race
   b. immanence of development
   c. autonomy of individual creation.
      It would also be necessary to criticize the various mechanical and vulgar materialistic interpretations of art.

II. Investigation of
   a. traditions of realism
   b. artists and art during past revolutionary periods
   c. the content of modern, especially abstract, art
   d. the interrelation of modern realistic arts (painting, cinema, literature)

III. Exposure of unacknowledged social and ideological bases of typical methods of art investigation
   a. connoisseurship and attribution
   b. formalistic analysis
   c. culture-historical (*geistesgeschichtliche*) analysis.

IV. Critique of official academic teaching of art-history, the "iconographic" methods of the Princeton scholars, historical formalism, general tendencies of archaeological research, etc.

V. Another important set of problems are those concerning modern architecture, functionalist aesthetic, architectural reformism, city-planning and housing, etc.[51]

At this point in time he gave these problems their due but most of his finished essays centered on medieval art, his other scholarly specialty. A book he was planning on *The Content of Modern Art: Studies in the Painting of the End of the Nineteenth Century from Manet to Munch* never came together.[52]

In 1946, as the full extent of the atrocities, the death camps and the atom bomb became clear, Schapiro, who had continued teaching and writing during World War II, worked up an essay for the October issue of the little magazine *View.* This time he closed in on *Crows in a Wheatfield,* thought to be Van Gogh's last painting before committing suicide.

Much as an artist would, Schapiro spoke to actuality by means of a single work of art. Isamu Noguchi did the cover design for that *View,* transforming one of his wall sculptures into a picture. Thin scaffolding set up around a bone-shape; tilting, sheer yellow planes brought short cheer. That Noguchi had voluntarily spent part of the war in an American internment camp for the Nisei was well-known, a fact the cover implied.[53] They had all been released. Letters spelled out the spread of life in French–V, I, E.

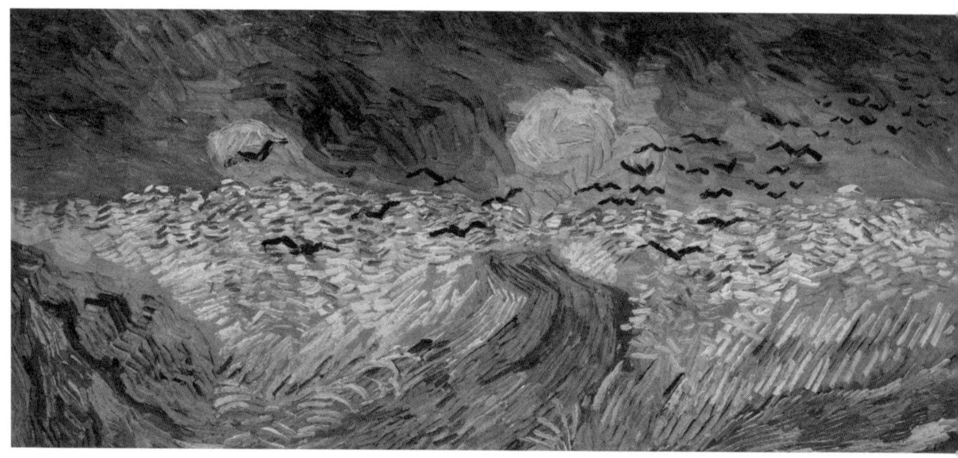

Vincent Van Gogh, *Crows in a Wheatfield,* 1890. The Van Gogh Museum, Amsterdam.

In *View* Schapiro's art history found a different platform. Charles Henri Ford had started the magazine during the war to gather the forces of the emigré European artists, writers and intellectuals together with their American counterparts, many of whom had

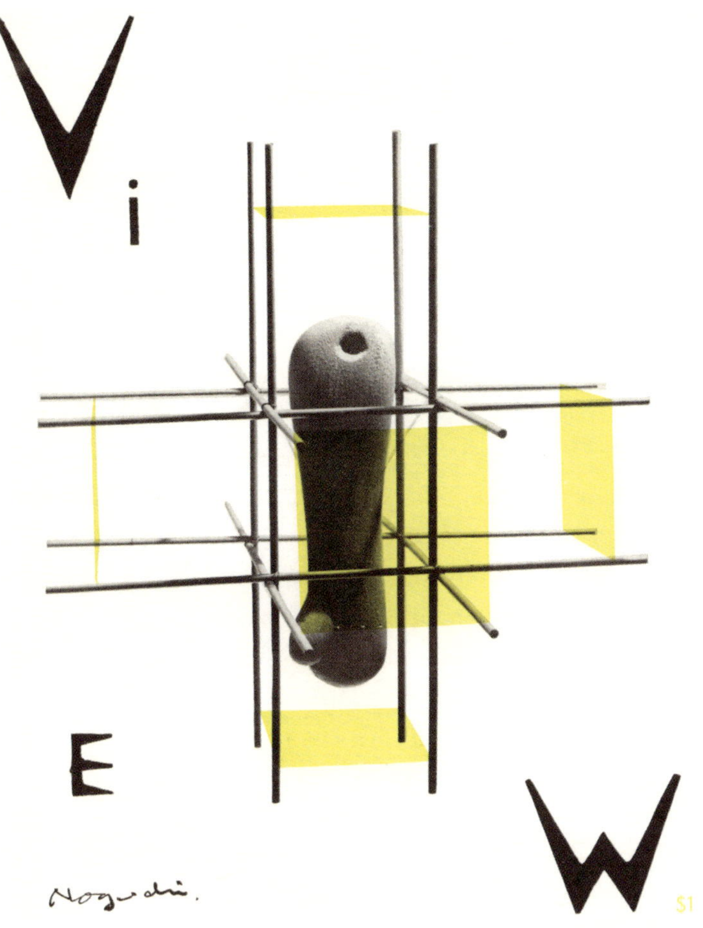

Isamu Noguchi, Cover, *View*, series VI, no. 5 (October 1946).

previously been living abroad. The Surrealists figured prominently on its pages, there with reviews of mathematical game theory, the writing of Wallace Stevens and Jean Genet and Marcel Duchamp's *infra-mince*. The combinations had kept avant-garde culture going, very unpredictably, watchful and wakeful.

View translated the "Circular Ruins" of J. L. Borges in January 1946, the story Borges had published in *Sur* in December 1940 as the war in Europe was escalating and those in Argentina around *Sur,* Borges included, were trying to combat the fascism mounting in the New World. The "Circular Ruins" summoned every resource; illusions grew atop allusions as Borges told the story about the dangers that overcame a magician who wanted to dream a man and insert him into reality. It ended suddenly: "First: (at the end of a long drought) a far-off cloud on a mountain peak, light as a bird; then, toward the south, the sky, pink as the gums of a leopard; then the clouds of smoke that rusted the metallic nights; after that the panick flight of the beasts."[54]

What did it mean to read these pages at war's end? *View* was clearly remaining on active alert. It sponsored a lecture by Sartre at Carnegie Hall in early March of 1946. It published the soldier Francis Lee's account of his visits to Picasso's studio just after the liberation of Paris. Lee had been the first American Picasso saw; they talked about the Gestapo's many visits to his studio; Picasso explained that he had had no truck with the officers wanting to do him favors but to the German enlisted men who came alone, he gave sketches. Lee looked at the paintings on the easel and concluded that Picasso was still absorbed by the horrors of the war.[55]

Into this *View* Schapiro's art history came and lent another hand. That summer of 1946, a reproduction of *Crows in a Wheatfield* hung in his office and it was absorbing him. His topic was not a casual choice. He approached Noguchi's move toward the bone. *Crows in a Wheatfield,* Schapiro told his reader, was a picture that expanded the frame horizontally to such a degree that, although the canvas was not large, it became too wide for a single person, or even two people, to see.[56] Instead of the expected march of perspective into depth, the spectator found wildly diverging roads and an unmanageable space flowing sideways and forward. The picture seemed to be asking that the viewer bring the stability usually provided by a vanishing point. Under these conditions, how to focus, or view? It was like discovering that an infernal fury lay unbidden deep inside the atom, or like the sense of utter destruction that overcame Gertrude Stein when she pondered the consequences of Cubism. Schapiro was pointing to the maelstrom in a bright field of ripe grain.

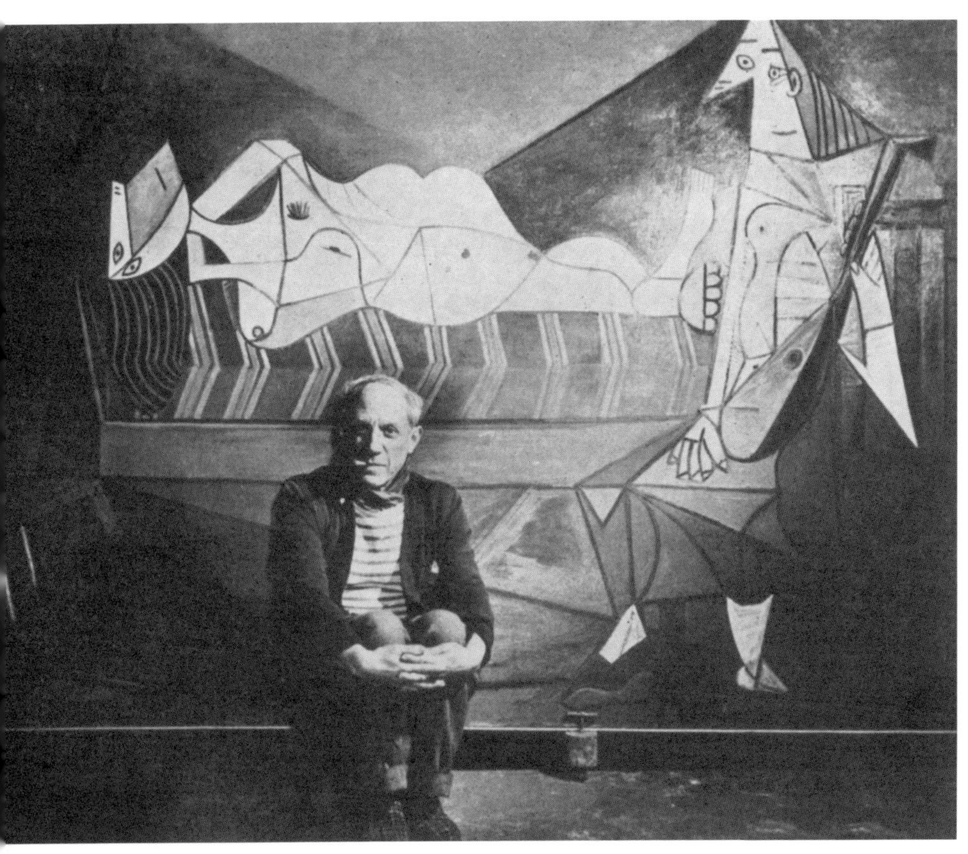

Francis Lee, Picasso in his Studio, *View*, series VI, nos. 2-3 (March-April 1946) p. 16.

He held onto its colors, counting them out one by one. He could see further into this field if he took the colors alone; he could see a life's force there, a vitality being expressed pictorially. Through the blue, yellow, brown and green, the painting mounted a resistance to full-out obliteration. But color was not working alone. Van Gogh, Schapiro emphasized, was attached to the entire reality of the countryside in which he lived. And while he painted, even at the last, his vision, his view forward, was fixed on his rustic, archaic world and its hues, until "the endless depth has been transposed into a sheer extension that exceeds the individual's glance and finally absorbs him."[57]

Was this, the essay's final sentence, so different in kind from the panick flight of beasts or the scene Jackson Pollock decided to

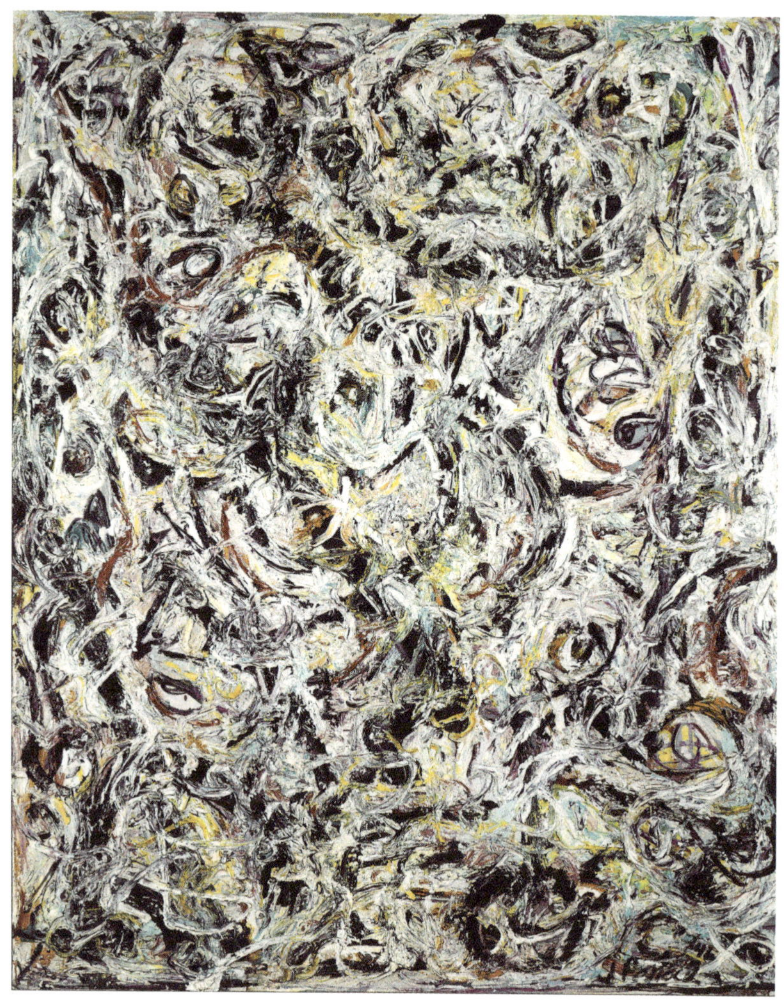

Jackson Pollock, *Eyes in the Heat*, 1946. The Solomon R. Guggenheim Foundation, Peggy Guggenheim Collection, Venice.

paint in the summer of 1946 where he mixed eyes into a field of pure heat?[58] The views before them all were fraught. In 1946 their mutual friend Willem de Kooning was stripping the color out of his own painting and naming one of them after Faulkner's novel *Light in August*. The previous August being the month when Hiroshima and Nagasaki had received the full hell of the atom bomb. But the materials Schapiro chose to parse and test in 1946 came from the modern art he had inherited, from Van Gogh's letters, from the study of psychology and from his own visual experience with the laws of perspective.

Schapiro's mind by then had taken in the dialectical negation being practiced by the Frankfurt School's Institute for Social Research, which had relocated from Germany to Columbia University in 1935; he knew Claude Lévi-Strauss and the other French emigrés who had gone to the New School for Social Research, setting up an Ecole Libre des Hautes Etudes in 1941. On his research trip to Europe in 1939 he had met Walter Benjamin, whom he failed to convince to depart immediately for America.[59] During the same trip, he had tried to meet Ludwig Wittgenstein in Cambridge, where Schapiro had gone to give a lecture on "Physicalism and Art." In that lecture, building on the theses Otto Neurath was developing for the study of sociology, he had raised the problem of logical structure in the statements typically used to study art—material descriptions, stylistic attributions, meaning statements broken down into iconographic, historical significance, logical significance, expression statements, geneological statements, space-time classifications and value judgments. Schapiro attacked the general vagueness in the field, yet noted that there could be no complete knowledge of the work of art. And emphasized that vagueness of language is not vagueness for the artist, for whom vague meaning is a precise value in a given place.[60]

Beginning in 1940 Schapiro was promising an essay on "Investigation and Criticism of the Arts" for the *Encyclopedia of Unified Science* being assembled by Rudolph Carnap, Otto Neurath and Charles Morris.[61] He was planning to transform the Cambridge lecture into a reflection on the relations between art and science—a basic problem for the evaluation and criticism of *science,* he thought—Schapiro's idea being to expose the methods of investigation in each and to account for their general differences and their possibilities. He was seeking out the processes, historical and phenomenological, through which to discover and know value in art.[62] He was never going to be satisfied with his effort to generalize them.

How then to know art? In 1942 Schapiro wrote to the artist Wolfgang Paalen à propos a survey on Dialectical Materialism just published in Paalen's review *Dyn*. It was a long and critical letter. He detailed the context in which he and his friends in the Philosophical Society, a group in close touch with the Vienna Circle and mainly interested in logic, mathematics and physics, had found dialectical materialism, as a rule, wanting. But so had his friends in the Trotskyite group:

> The mere assertion of actuality and of a turning-point in contemporary thought proves nothing, except perhaps the desire for actuality and a turning-point. One doesn't document actuality and intellectual turning points with monotonous "nos" ... For my part I have read nothing in contemporary political and social analysis that can be set beside the writings of the great Marxists [Marx, Engels, Lenin, Luxemburg, Trotsky].[63]

He lectured Paalen further on dia[lectical] mat[erialism] and then toward the end said about Dewey, "he wants a theory that will satisfy the functions that Engels and Lenin thought would be satisfied by diamat [sic] e.g.–adequate to deal with process, change, quality in its gradations, emergence and discontinuities." At the same time he was careful to take his own distance from Dewey's social writings, calling them "pettifogging liberalism" and branding them, too, vague. All that said, before and after this letter, Schapiro's own intellectual instruments remained by and large those he had taken from the pragmatists. He looked to see sight. The ways of seeing he found would be individual, empirical and historical in nature, and they embraced the things beyond images, the vagueness, the things that kept him writing in pursuit. In 1946 he was bringing all of this experience to the *Crows in a Wheatfield* without saying so.

Thirty-five years later, Jacques Derrida lectured at Columbia on Van Gogh's paintings of shoes. Derrida had gone to great lengths to put forward another kind of meditation on statements, anti-logical in the extreme, and had cast Schapiro aside, by name, as a worthless philosophical naif. Schapiro met the charge head-on. He stood up. Rather than say "no," or embark on a swift rebuke or even a rebuttal, much to the surprise of those present he simply said to Derrida, "I am a student of John Dewey and I believe in the truth," leaving Derrida to ascertain what exactly that reticence now meant.[64]

That same fall of 1946, not so far away, in Rhode Island, Alexander Dorner, the visionary German museum director who had emigrated to New York eight years before, diagrammed the modern picture. According to Dorner the modern picture was drawing away from views of three-dimensional reality, dissolving outward as the energies of human experience produced new transformations in time. Form could never be timeless because life would never be static, never repeat.[65] Even more radically, Dorner proposed to detach the term "art" from this movement, rendering the question that had haunted modern art—"Is it art?"— simply moot.[66]

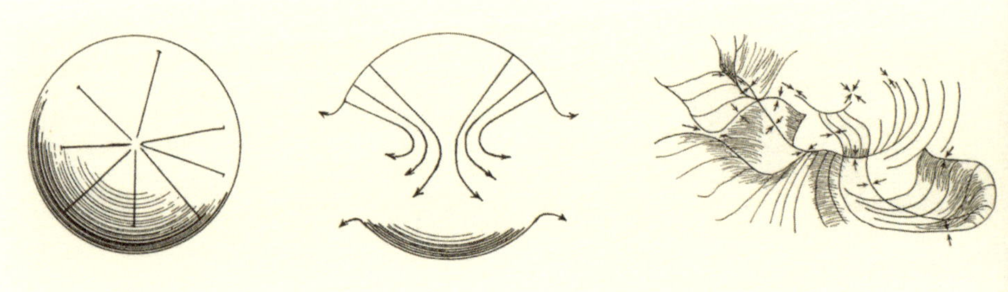

Alexander Dorner, Diagram of the Dissolution of the Western Picture of Three-Dimensional Reality, *The Way Beyond 'Art'* (New York: Wittenborn, 1947) p. 229.

Dorner had been working on these ideas for some time. In 1931 he had published an article in the *Cahiers d'Art* on the meaning of abstract art in relation to the scientific discoveries of space-time. Dorner extrapolated, envisioned abstract form to be the means to arrive at an end that was not an end-in-itself. He too saw the picture frame ceding its boundaries. He wrote of the potential to be found in the new physics and film.[67] The book that Dorner was finishing in 1946, *The Way Beyond 'Art'*, followed from these ideas but it went further, incorporating more. It would be dedicated to John Dewey, who wrote the preface for it.

Dewey thought *The Way Beyond 'Art'* especially important because it called attention to the presence of a great, moving intellectual transformation that was taking everyone away from the fixed certainties upon which science and civilization itself had up until then been based: in science, laws were changing into statistical probabilities; in philosophy, a new respect for process was making its way into the concept of knowledge. Dewey chalked this up to a new emphasis on events and facts. "'Event,'" he wrote, "is the aspect of [our knowing] which comes out of, which proceeds, from a total process, whose other aspect is 'fact,' that which is done, finished (in a relative sense) while event and fact enter together as inscriptions of new events and new things to be done."[68] Events and facts brought philosophy into a dynamic, a life in which the artist participated too, seeing and helping others to see. Dewey was not so grandiose as to designate it as the present or the future, as if those things existed apart from a person; he spoke instead of the large vitality and community of life. And he seconded Dorner's call to give time itself, history, a deeper meaning. Like the writers at *View*, they did not have to say that this time of theirs came on the heels of the world's worst-ever war.

The Way Beyond 'Art' came out in 1947 in the landmark series of modern artists' writing being published by George Wittenborn; consequently this first edition of Dorner's book took the work of Herbert Bayer as its centerpiece. But Dorner's concerns remained broad; they issued as much if not more from his experience as director of the Hannover Landesmuseum. There Dorner had worked to make installations that returned works of art to their historically specific settings by means of period rooms. In 1925 he had commissioned El Lissitzky to design just such a room for the art of the absolute present; El Lissitzky had produced an Abstract Cabinet with walls of corrugated tin painted in alternating bars of grey and black, a white line running straight down the top of each pleat. This pattern set up an abstract field, an optical electricity, to host the new geometric reductions in painting being made by Picasso, Léger and Mondrian, among others.

The Abstract Cabinet joined the Landesmuseum's sequence of period rooms. Dorner was using his sense of art history to make

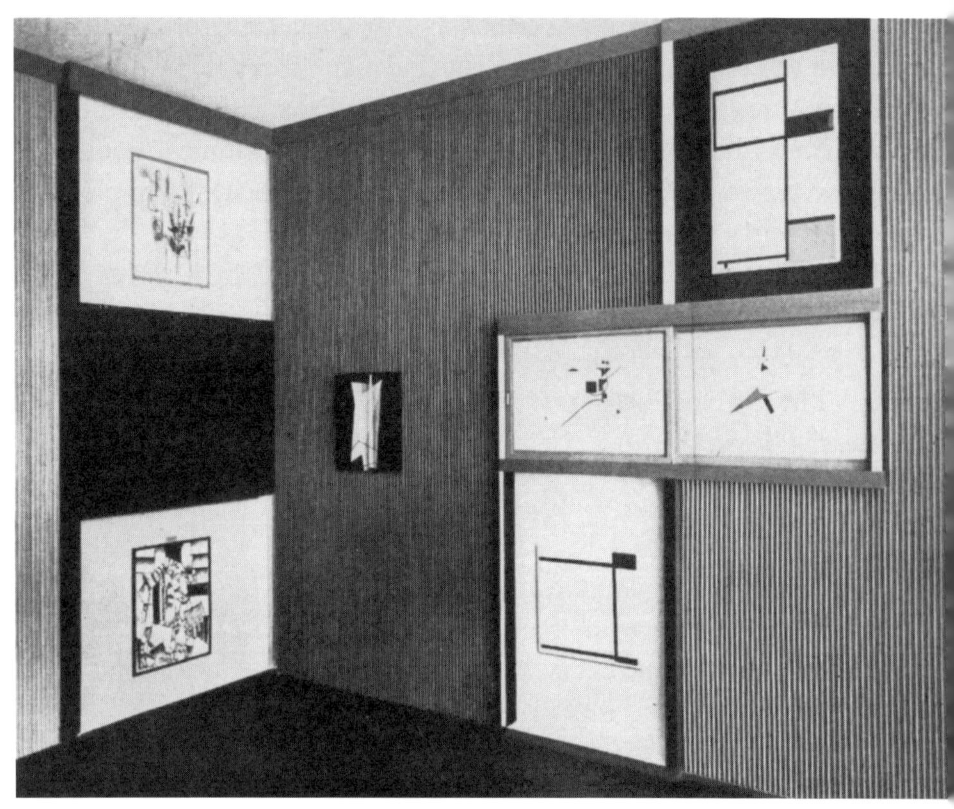

El Lissitzky, *Abstract Cabinet*, 1925 (now destroyed). Hannover Landesmuseum, illustrated in Dorner, *The Way Beyond 'Art,'* p. 115.

what he called "a living museum," one meant to keep extending.[69] When Malevich's widow was able to smuggle his remaining abstract work out of Russia, Dorner gave it safe haven; when the Nazis in their turn deemed such art degenerate, he helped smuggle it out of Germany. In 1935 Alfred Barr did his part to help them by taking away Suprematist compositions rolled into his umbrella.[70] The continuum found itself adrift. Dorner's rooms of modern art would soon be closed and destroyed by the state; his work would be known afterward only through a few photographs. The Room for Our Time that he had asked László Moholy-Nagy to design in 1930 was to have included two film projections, one for abstract film and the other for documentary, along with displays of the latest photography and design.

In the United States Alfred Barr would help him get settled. On his own Dorner discovered a kindred spirit in Dewey, who had, because of his work with Dr. Albert Barnes, given the museum a similar role to play in *Art as Experience*. Yet neither the Landesmuseum nor the Barnes Foundation came to have much of a public profile in the years to come. For his part, Dorner held the post of director at the Museum of the Rhode Island School of Design until 1941 when anti-German sentiment there forced him out; subsequently at Brown University he would teach and plan to integrate art with science, industrial design and the long lines of history, but he had no place to experiment with display. The book was part of an attempt to do more.

In 1946 Dorner was still imagining a museum becoming a powerhouse, producing new energies.[71] In 1947 he proposed a plan for galleries at the Graduate School of Design at Harvard that would have had no fixed walls at all. Later he dreamed of a space where the history of art could be shown as nothing more than an interpenetrating field of weightless forces—"complete inner flexibility, a cobweb of massless interacting members so thin, so light, that it is less a closed permanent form than an action, a process."[72] After his death in 1957 another, not so Bayer-centric edition of *The Way Beyond 'Art'* was brought out and in the next decades it would come to inspire many curators in Europe. But these dreams would not find root in the United States.

West of the Atlantic other theaters of operation were prevailing. They were the ones to broker modern art's American history after the second World War; they ensured that a framed, formalist orthodoxy of abstract art became the image regime and fixed standard for a modern aesthetic, traditional in that it was based on the work of painters and sculptors. In 1943 Barr brought out *What Is Modern Painting?*, a short introductory guide that answered its own question. Barr produced another diagram showing a linear composition lifting from the background of Whistler's portrait of his mother, a prediction and apparent confirmation of the modern geometric picture.[73] Abstraction seemed both logical and inevitable in such a scenario, the product of a deduction and at the same time a prime mover. But it was better to avoid questions.

And so it was Barr's first demonstration, *Cubism and Abstract Art,* that became the authoritative version of modern art's abstraction. The catalogue stayed in print after the war, to be used for decades as a college textbook, its view of modern art's foundations projected throughout the Museum of Modern Art's growing permanent collection. Repetition and stasis won the arguments over definitions. When it appeared, *The Marriage of Reason and Squalor* by Frank Stella was seen to fall quite naturally into the line of descent.

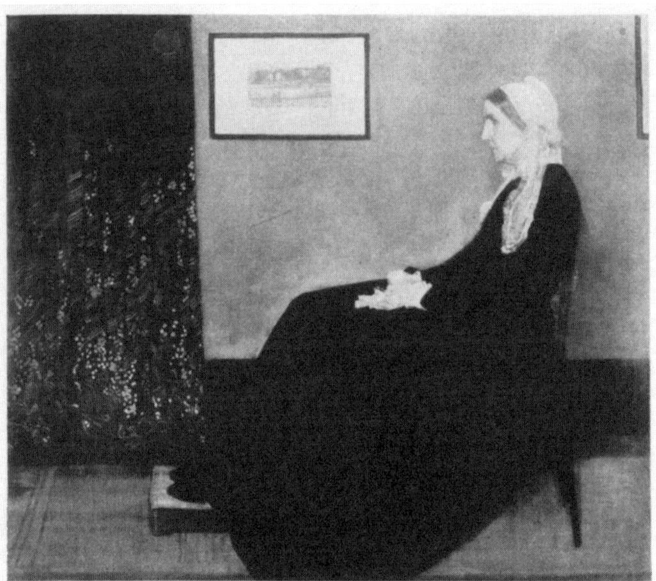

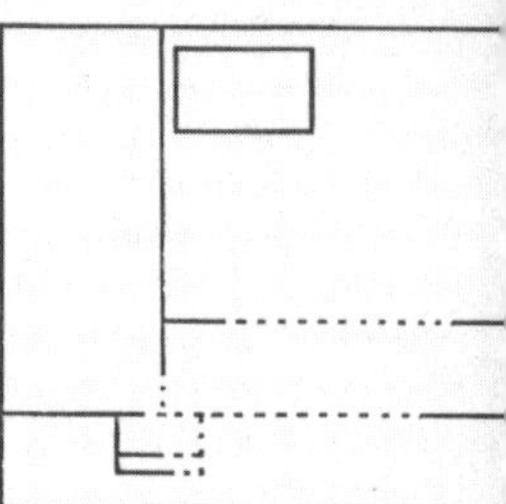

Alfred Barr Jr., Diagram of Whistler's Composition, *What is Modern Painting?* (New York: The Museum of Modern Art, 1943) p. 12.

The establishment of an orthodox abstraction was helped immeasurably by a wave of confirming art criticism. "Content," the young critic Clement Greenberg had declared in 1939, "is to be dissolved so completely into form that the work of art or literature cannot be reduced in whole or in part to anything not itself."[74] The idea came to be taken as an edict. When Greenberg collected some of his best reviews into *Art and Culture* in 1961, that

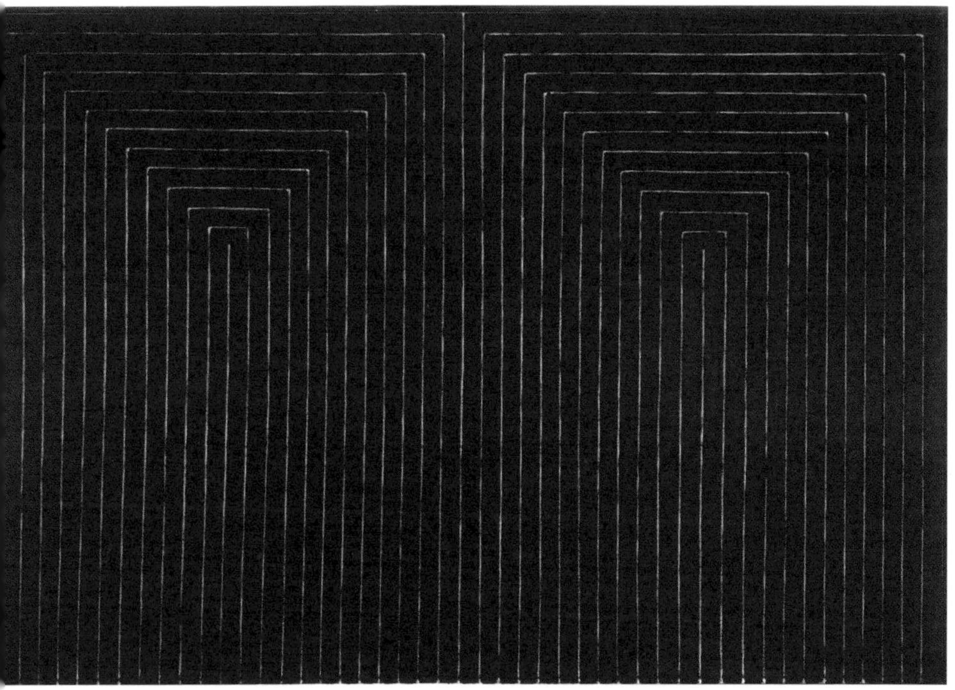

Frank Stella, *The Marriage of Reason and Squalor, II,* 1959. The Museum of Modern Art, New York.

book too would become a standard reference and its success would be symptomatic of other things to come. Criticism, or more correctly, the catalogue essay or exhibition review, was to become the brief, and the only brief, for writing about art of the present. Larger historical forces and other realities, things not-paintings and not-sculptures, things not exhibited, were ushered away from the big stage. Objects were given priority.

In the wings, something else was stirring. An equally, if not more powerful, and completely anterior image, the mirror reflection, was being used to erect a very different kind of regime for modern objects and subjects. One saw them this way, together, in advertisements. These mirror images kept the human figure intact. They implied a spectator falling for the illusion, instinctively conforming to it, as if the mirror could produce the figure before it rather than the other way around. The ad promoted its product together with a way of infatuated seeing that became almost automatic in mid-century

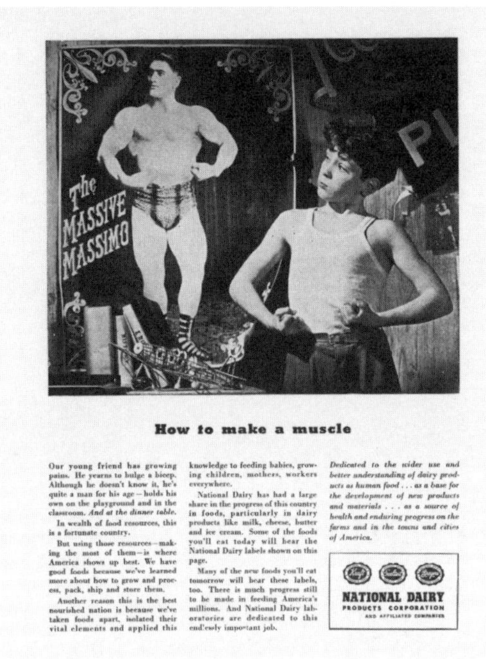

Advertisement, National Dairy Products Corporation, Marshall McLuhan, *The Mechanical Bride: Folklore of Industrial Man* (New York: Vanguard, 1951) p. 142.

America. More than that, the ad was installing its own set of baselines and expectations into pictures generally.

The ensuing dance of identification on the pages of magazines and newspapers would drive an entire industrial economy forward. It came to seem stable. It also became tough competition for any other image coming near. In the summer of 1937 Robert Capa's photograph of a Spanish Republican soldier being shot dead on the battlefield was itself assaulted by the pitch from a hair tonic on the pages of *LIFE*.

As for the older pragmatic perspectives and ways, they were overshadowed, or assimilated too well, carried along by work that did not refer to them per se, visible in skips and starts. Time marched on. The ascendant image regimes, the abstractions and the mirrors, would soon enough come under scrutiny, their modernities defined and parsed critically, phenomenologically, semiotically, psychoanalytically, if not historically; subsequent attempts to move the picture into

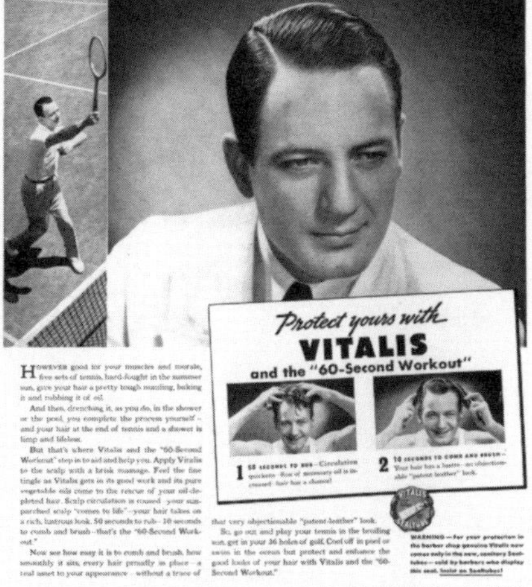

LIFE

Vol. 3, No. 2

JULY 12, 1937

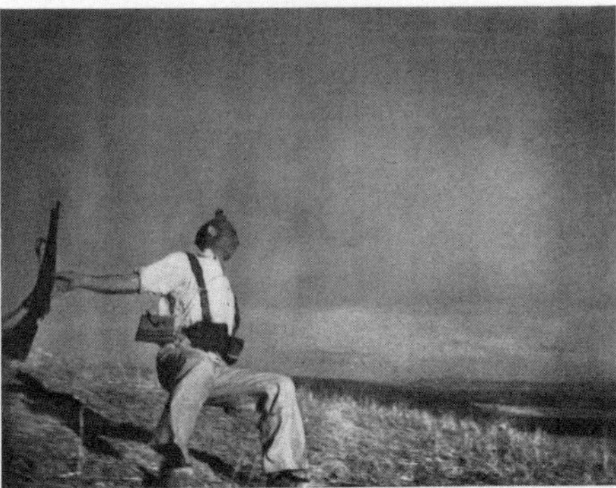

ROBERT CAPA'S CAMERA CATCHES A SPANISH SOLDIER THE INSTANT HE IS DROPPED BY A BULLET THROUGH THE HEAD IN FRONT OF CORDOBA

DEATH IN SPAIN: THE CIVIL WAR HAS TAKEN 500,000 LIVES IN ONE YEAR

On July 17 the Spanish Civil War will be one year old. In that time it has brought Death to 500,000 Spaniards, has shattered such ancient cities as Madrid, Toledo, Bilbao, Irun and Durango, has kept Europe in a state of jitters.

When the war started, most U. S. citizens looked on the Loyalists as a half-crazy, irresponsible, murderous scum that had turned on its honorable betters. A year of war has taught the U. S. more of Spain.

The ruling classes of Spain were probably the world's worst bosses—irresponsible, arrogant, vain, ignorant, shiftless and incompetent. Some 20,000 landlords owned 50% of the land. They did not give their field hands modern machinery or their land modern irrigation. They refused to rent unused land to landless peasants for fear of giving the peasants dangerous ideas of ownership. The land was only about 25% efficient and much of it was idle. And Spain's mineral resources, among the greatest in Europe, lay almost entirely unexploited. The aristocracy of Spain was still living on the interest on wealth brought home from the Americas by the gold fleets in the 16th Century.

To the 20,000 landlords, add 21,000 Army officers, more than twice the total of British Army officers. There was one officer for every six privates, one general for every 150 men. For every $5 spent on soldiers' pay, food, barracks, ammunition, officers got $10 in pay—25% of the national budget. The national law made officers semisacred. Just for pushing a policeman of the swank Civil Guard, six Americans got six months in jail in 1935.

Add to the 41,000 landlords and officers, 100,000 clergy, the most top-heavy Church hierarchy in the world, next to Tibet. These also were paid by the State. The Church, with its enormous wealth, naturally took a capitalist's position. It was up to its neck in politics. Peasants were told that to vote against the Conservatives was usually a mortal sin. The Church was in charge of Spanish education. Result: the Spanish people were 45% illiterate. The reason for the civil war was simply that the people of Spain had fired their bosses for flagrant incompetence and the bosses had refused to be fired.

For a new movie of the Spanish war from the Government side, turn page.

Robert Capa, "Loyalist Militiaman at the Moment of Death, Cerro Muriano, September 5, 1936," *LIFE* (July 12, 1937) pp. 18-19. From the pages of *LIFE*. *LIFE* and the *LIFE* logo are registered trademarks of TI Gotham Inc. used under license.

other territories were made and sometimes succeeded. Imperial wars continued, revolutions persisted, technologies evolved, industries rose and fell, men were launched into space, people came and went. By 1960 John Dewey, Gertrude Stein and Alexander Dorner were dead. The present pressed ahead.

The chase continued and changed course. In 1970 John Hightower was brought in from the New York State Council on the Arts to become the director of the Museum of Modern Art. As he arrived, domestic and foreign conflict roiled the country, protests against the Vietnam War had turned deadly, riots ignited in the decay of the inner cities, equal civil rights were far from guaranteed. Facts and events were in such upheaval that they were forcing a general re-examination of the whole. Hightower laid out an agenda that reset the mission of the Museum. He began by proposing that it use its collections as a fixed point from which to address the human concerns of the next decade. He stressed the need to develop better educational programs that would involve more of the community and that would address the senses as well as the mind. In his memos and press releases, he was speaking Dewey's language.[75] He set his sights outside. Hightower would not be able to realize these projects; in less than two years he would be gone. But these were the policies that made it possible for Kynaston McShine to curate *Information* in the summer of 1970.

Information has since become legendary for the level of its ambition and independence: it sought to comprehend the full scale of this present, including everything that Barr had hoped to cut from the discussion of modern art. In 1970 the everything was called *politics*, a rich word that spoke to the entire life of the *polis* and called it to account. McShine took the occasion to put together an experiment, a politics that looked forward internationally and used any and all means of exhibition to reach viewers. The catalogue cover showed an array of old and brand new communications media—a Kodak Instamatic, a touch-tone phone, a homing pigeon; the inside was largely given over to an anthology of artists' pages and statements. His catalogue essay introduced them and took stock:

> The material presented by the artists is considerably varied, and also spirited, if not rebellious-which is not very surprising, considering the general social,

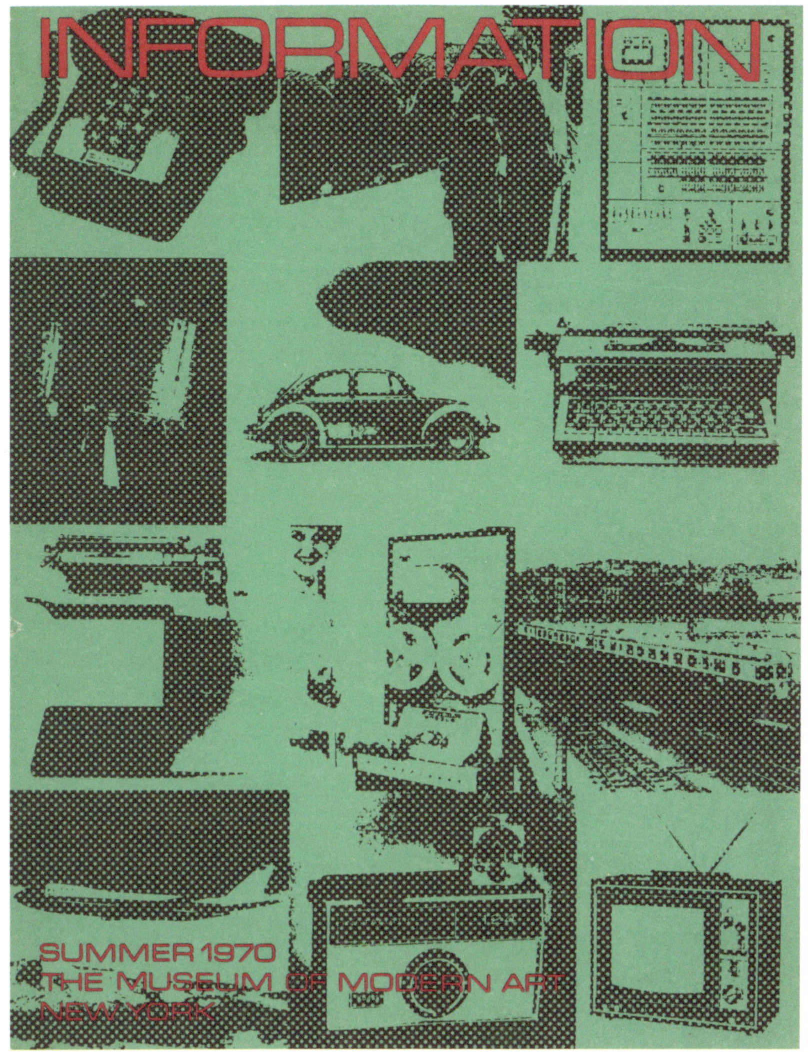

Cover, *Information*, ed. Kynaston McShine (New York: The Museum of Modern Art, 1970).

political and economic crises that are almost universal phenomena of 1970. If you are an artist in Brazil, you know of at least one friend who is being tortured; if you are one in Argentina, you probably have had a neighbor who has been in jail for having long hair, or for not being "dressed" properly; and if you are living in the United States, you may fear that you will be shot at,

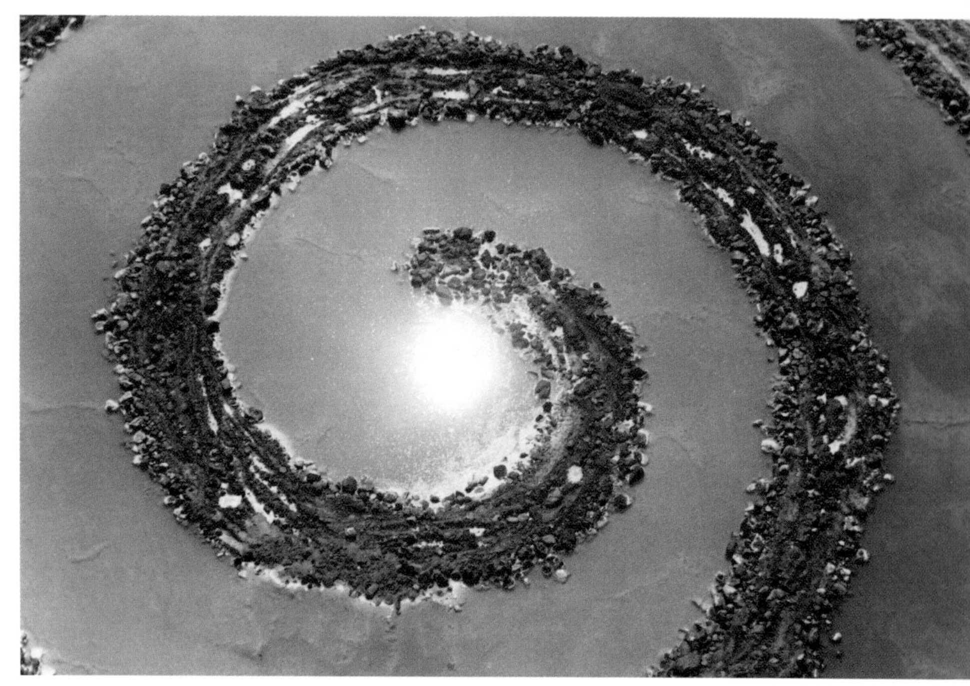

Robert Smithson, *Spiral Jetty*, Rozelle Point, Great Salt Lake, Utah, April 1970. Photo: Gianfranco Gorgoni.

either in the universities, your bed, or more formally in Indochina. It may seem too inappropriate, if not absurd, to get up in the morning, walk into a room, and apply dabs of paint from a little tube to a square of canvas. What can you as a young artist do that seems relevant and meaningful?[76]

Robert Smithson submitted the documentation for his project *Asphalt Rundown,* in which he poured asphalt to no end, no road, down a quarry slope in Cava di Selce near Rome. That, at any rate, was his contribution to the catalogue as it went to press. For the show itself, he submitted photographs of the just-completed *Spiral Jetty* in the Great Salt Lake of Utah.

They found company in John Giorno's bank of twelve telephones where the visitor could Dial-a-Poem and then be surprised by a voice—taped by a known poet like Allen Ginsberg and Frank O'Hara or a better-known radical like the Yippie Abbie Hoffman and the Black Panthers Eldridge Cleaver and Bobby Seale (the program was rich and changed daily). The artist Hélio Oiticica made nests for the visitors: "it's important that the ideas of environment, participation, sensorial experiments, etc., be not limited to objectal solutions: they should propose a development of life-acts and not a representation... they exist as a plan for a practice... an open plan that can be expanded, gr o o o ow," the artist explained.[77] Hans Haacke came with a poll asking "Would the fact that Governor Rockefeller has not denounced President Nixon's Indochina policy be a reason for you not to vote for him in November?" The Art Workers' Coalition poster protesting the My Lai massacre went up on the wall; so did Robert Rauschenberg's poster for the first Earth Day and Andy Warhol's proclamation: "In The Future Everybody Will Be Famous For Fifteen Minutes."[78] The information was, in its way, current, volatile and activist.

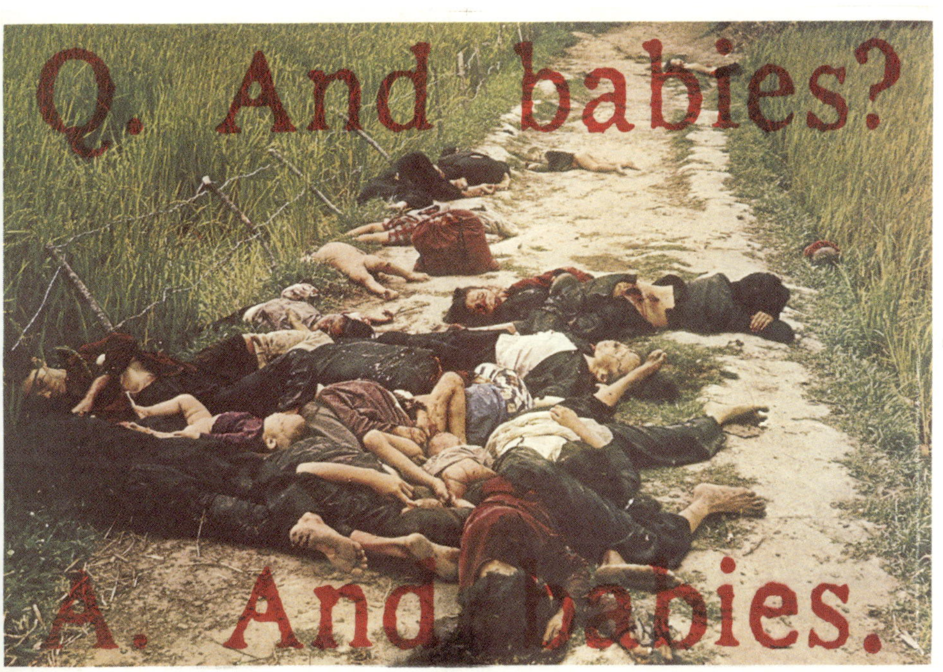

Art Workers' Coalition (Frazier Dougherty, Jon Hendricks, Irving Petlin), *Q: And babies?* 1970. The Museum of Modern Art, New York.

For Hightower *Information* was nothing more or less than an exhibition of free speech where artists had expressed their concerns about the obstacles they saw standing in the way of art or life. He pointed to the war in Vietnam, symbolic of all kinds of cultural excess. He agreed with those artists who felt that death pervaded almost everything Americans did. "At the same time," he said bluntly as the exhibition drew criticism, "artists are saying, through some of the technological media, that art is not property; it is not solely an adornment; it is not an object to be either revered like an icon or traded like a commodity. In many ways, though this is what art has become, and the Museum has played a role in its treatment as such. Both art and man are diminished." Art, he felt, deserved better. It deserved more life.[79]

The question about life went together with a dread about the course the present was taking. Many artists, Smithson for one, found strange guidance in a book written by an art historian, the Pre-Columbian expert George Kubler. Kubler gave them no security when he wrote: "Actuality is...the interchronic pause when nothing is happening. It is the void between events." Yet Smithson quoted these lines with approval; he seemed himself to live in them. He also noted that Kubler had suggested that the example of physical, not biological science, was more appropriate to the discussion of art's particular nature.[80] The example of physical science would lead Smithson to the *Jetty* and, he reported, to the sight of the voids beyond formal thought—somehow still cupping a landscape: "It was as if the mainland oscillated with waves and pulsations, and the lake remained rock still. The shore of the lake became the edge of the sun, a boiling curve, an explosion rising into a fiery prominence. Matter collapsing into the lake mirrored in the shape of a spiral. No sense wondering about classifications and categories, there were none."[81]

New Haven

Kubler's book, *The Shape of Time*, had appeared in 1962. To make his way forward, he had chosen to take up the mental instruments he had found in mathematics and the new physics, especially the signal models from electro-dynamics. In many ways he was continuing to work with the pragmatic trajectories of reasoning, but his own turn toward this kind of thinking had been set in motion by his teacher, a Frenchman who had come from the Sorbonne to Yale University for a few months each year, starting in 1933, to help expand its fledgling program in art history. His name was Henri Focillon. Actuality had been the question that haunted him as he lay on his deathbed in early 1943. "*Qu'est-ce que c'est l'actualité?*"[82] Focillon left Kubler with the question. It led Kubler to his book, where he took it to the lighthouse.

Kubler did not presume to answer the question. In lieu of fresh certainties he offered a sweep of examples. Were they catalysts? Initially he had imagined a lighthouse going completely black. Then he came to a formulation he liked better, and that, perhaps because it was lengthy, Smithson would only partly cite:

> Actuality is when the lighthouse is dark between flashes: it is the instant between the ticks of the watch: it is a void interval slipping forever through time: the rupture between past and future: the gap at the poles of the revolving magnetic field, infinitesimally small but ultimately real. It is the interchronic pause when nothing is happening. It is the void between events.
>
> Yet the instant of actuality is all we ever can know directly. The rest of time emerges only in signals relayed to us at this instant by innumerable stages and by unexpected bearers. These signals are like kinetic energy stored until the moment of notice when the mass descends along some portion of its path to the center

of the gravitational system. One may ask why these old signals are not actual. The nature of a signal is that its message is neither here nor now, but there and then.[83]

This was evolving into another order of information entirely.

Focillon had published a book, *The Life of Forms in Art,* in 1934, which was just as eloquent in a different way, building upon analyses taken from linguistics and the natural sciences. Kubler had been so inspired that while still a student he translated the book into English. In *The Life of Forms in Art,* Focillon saw form to be akin to matter; it was an idea that did *not* separate form from life but rather bound it to life's very dynamic of metamorphosis; he saw formal change to be a dialectic or experimental process, something *made* physical: "touch," he wrote memorably, "is structure."[84] Henri Bergson's philosophy of creative evolution informed this version of life but equally present was the idea that form was bound inextricably to the world, and that there was a world too of form, in form.

In his own mind Focillon did not see this way of thinking as having begun with a "system." When he wrote to Yale to make the formal argument for art history's place in university knowledge, he placed it firmly inside what was then understood to be the discipline of history.[85] And himself? Focillon would be named to the Collège de France in 1938, but he continued to teach in New Haven for a few months each year. By then Focillon also had stepped, completely consciously, into the public tide of his time. Time and tide turned him toward the things he did not know yet.

It was the Dreyfus Affair of 1898 that radicalized Focillon but only after World War I did he begin to speak to history as an intellectual. When the League of Nations started, an International Institute for Cultural Cooperation became part of its platform of operations, Bergson himself at the head. As the Institute evolved in the late twenties, the writer Paul Valéry together with Focillon took over Bergson's role, the two of them chairing what came to be called The Permanent Committee on Arts and Letters in 1930 and instituting a range of programs that set topics before invited international groups of thinkers, writers, musicians and architects. "Our role is not one of study or pure speculation," they wrote. "He who says cooperation says action."

Focillon and Valéry wanted to put forward the idea of a League of Spirit, or Mind (Société des Esprits) to accompany the activities of the League of Nations (known in French as the Société des Nations). This involved thinking about coordinating the laws on copyright that protected the rights of authors; it involved strategies for harnessing the new media of radio and cinema; it involved international exchanges between universities.[86] Immediately Focillon went on record to say that mass culture and the culture of quality should not be placed in mindless opposition, and that the machine was part and parcel of the new culture.[87] Focillon's yearly course at Yale needs to be understood with these greater purposes of international understanding and collaboration in mind.

The Permanent Committee hosted Conversations and Open Letters throughout the thirties, taking on topics—Goethe, the Future of Culture, the Future of the European Spirit, Art and Reality, Art and the State, Europe and Latin America, the Next Future of Letters, Towards a New Humanism. In 1933 it sponsored a public exchange of letters between Albert Einstein and Sigmund Freud on the lingering and ominous question "Why War?" Others who answered the call of the Permanent Committee included Bela Bartòk, Johan Huizinga, Aldous Huxley, Alfonso de Reyes, Marie Curie, Thomas Mann and Le Corbusier.

This order of work would change the scale of Focillon's *engagement* and his art historical thinking; it would introduce the world to his stage and bring a host of extramural concepts into his *Life of Forms*. Its effects would echo later through Kubler's meditation on actuality in the *The Shape of Time*:

> The segmentation of history is still an arbitrary and conventional matter, governed by no verifiable

> conception of historical entities and their durations. Now and in the past, most of the time the majority of people live by borrowed ideas and upon traditional accumulations, yet at every moment the fabric is being undone and a new one is woven to replace the old, while from time to time the whole pattern shakes and quivers, settling into new shapes and figures. These processes of change are all mysterious uncharted regions where the traveler soon loses direction and stumbles in darkness. The clues to guide us are very few indeed: perhaps the jottings and sketches of architects and artists, put down in the heat of imagining a form, or the manuscript *brouillons* of poets and musicians, crisscrossed with erasures and corrections, are the hazy coast lines of this dark continent of the "now," where the impress of the future is received by the past.[88]

Echoes have origins as fleeting as flame, or swallowtail, as passing as they are factual. In 1937 Focillon, as part of his contribution to the meeting on the Next Future of Letters, spoke of the industrial advances in the nineteenth century. With Balzac in mind, he spoke of the inhuman comedy of the railroad and the way it seemed to produce things as a luminous, fugitive vision, full of sudden movement. The work of Balzac and the Impressionists had likewise been affected by industrialization, he said. When he spoke of the present, his tone changed.

> We find ourselves facing ever more violent news today. The stability, the resilence, of the antique halls of justice is being shaken and pierced through. Distant voices sing inside lamps. Life in toto is inscribed on a screen. Why should the mind turn away in order to stay faithful to an old structure of space-time? The author is not set before his milieu as if before some rock, on which he carves an inscription; he lives in his milieu and with it, he is bathed, and it is precisely because he

> collaborates with it that he is able in turn to give it a hitherto unpublished, and durable, form.[89]

The arrival of World War II, which in Europe officially began in September 1939, derailed the efforts of the League and the Permanent Committee. By October Focillon was in the United States both to teach at Yale and to begin a mission on behalf of the French state to rally support for the Allied cause, for the United States would not enter that war until the bombing of Pearl Harbor in December 1941. Each fall in New Haven, Focillon had made a practice of giving a cycle of public lectures at Yale: in 1937 he chose to focus on the churches of Spain, especially those close to the raging battles of the Spanish Civil War. "Timely," said the *Yale Daily News*, in its abbreviated, gentlemanly way, "since the problems of Spanish civilization are of great interest to the world at large."[90] In the fall of 1939, the battle lines now moving from another direction entirely toward France, Focillon chose to speak of Manet, beginning with Manet and Spain, followed by Manet the Portraitist, the figure of the Woman, and the subjects of Modern Life and *Plein-Air*.[91] In January 1940 he submitted his final version of the art history curriculum proposal to the university.[92] It would, in effect, teach an art history of the world in real time. He began by stating that the purpose of art history was not at all to carve out an existence in splendid isolation.

Art history at Yale was to be combined into the entire teaching of the university, contributing both to the formation of the student's culture and to his training in the ways of solid, scientific research, meaning thereby the formation of the *savant*, both expert and intellectual. Useful too, Focillon noted, for artists. A freshman taking the introductory courses would be given an essential part of a humanist's education. This meant taking all four of them:

> An Introduction to the Study of Fine Arts
> An Introduction to Architecture
> Methodology: Method of Research and Art Criticism
> Museography: Museum Management

The upper levels of instruction were divided by historical periods or regions according to the ways the discipline had at that time evolved. Europe, Asia, North and South America were all included. The teaching of Antiquity made a special point of Mesopotamia and Persia, where Yale was conducting archaeological excavations. These upper levels of art history often incorporated existing courses taught in other departments. Focillon's was a transdisciplinary vision of a field. But there was more: each class was scheduled to meet for three hours each week; two of those hours, Focillon thought, could focus directly on the material while the third hour could be used to bring out a particular question rising out of the presentation, one that imposed itself by virtue of its own merit or its current significance, its *actualité*.

Focillon envisioned the introductory Methodology course as a series of lectures. In January of 1940 he gave the first series of seven, open to all, at least initially, in the Yale Art Gallery. In them he charted the breadth and depth of the field as he understood it. Kubler was there.[93] The lectures were heading beyond the scope of *The Life of Forms in Art*, for like his fellow historians, Focillon was taking his thinking to the social sciences. Art history, as he now conceived it, was the study of *relations* that put art into contact with material that was geographic, ethnic, sociological, economic, philosophical. These did not converge simultaneously to make the work of art an automatic effect; the molecules of data were never stable and the work of art was itself capable of creating more, new historical data of further consequence. It could go on to constitute historical data in and of itself, not only for nascent works of art but for life and humanity. It had already created sociological forms, faiths, beliefs, economic conditions, geographic conditions and families of minds. He told his students to drop the idea of history as "`background`" and to see instead "`historic foundations.`"

This much was fundamental: the work of art existed as both a fact and an object with the power to exist in continuity. But a fact, he told them, is actually a point of contact between many fields. As such, this history was not the study of insular tradition; rather, it was a science without fixed laws. Focillon did not shield his students from the other

Method = technique of the mind. pre-1940?
Measurement = a reasoning : {observation and experiment
Object of study: work of art — a fact in space/time.

Where –
When –
Why –
How →
myths
nostalgias } efforts to break outside the circle of time.

Form = visibility, tactility, tangibility of the object.
the graph of an activity.
Specific organization of forms = style.
Style: 1) experimental/archaic
2) classic / mise au point,
3) mannerism / refinement
often equals academicism.
4) baroque / renewal, defiance,
Indissolubility of form/matter.
Technique ~ not a trade. Prolongation of individual life of artist, created by him.
e.g. photography: its materials are movement and light.
History of art the most complete of the historical disciplines, since it rejoins the natural sciences via the instruments of observation & experiment.

George Kubler, Notecard Summing up Focillon's Lectures. Circa 1940, inscribed later in Kubler's hand. Kubler Papers, Sterling Memorial Library, Manuscripts and Archives Collections, Yale University.

kinds of art history undertaken by Heinrich Wölfflin, Alois Riegl, Aby Warburg, Emile Mâle and Erwin Panofsky. He spoke to them in equal measure about Descartes, Bergson and phenomenology. The discipline as he conceived it had great capacity.[94] It too was plunged into the mobile structure of time, the diversity of movement and the play of metamorphoses, the *freedom* in form that *The Life of Forms* had begun to chart.[95] In 1941 he would pick up the threads of this teaching, but his health was failing. Although he again made notes for a lecture cycle divided into three parts, The World of Facts, The World of Forms, The Life, also a World, of the Spirit, he seems not to have given them. He would have concluded with a philosophy of freedom: "we are looking to unlock the network, to animate it, to make forces play out there—if opposed in principle they will find not their pacification but a sovereign state, there in the drama of the work of art. The more complex the mix, the more we are free."[96]

As he put forth these thoughts in America, Focillon was working for France. He had been redoubling his efforts for the resistance when France fell to the Germans in June 1940. Focillon had gotten the news while on his trip to South America. He had written about learning Paris had fallen as the foothills of the Andes rose before him. That summer he wrote an essay "To Our Friends in Argentina," which was printed in the Rio de Janeiro newspaper, speaking of the historical forces of fascism facing them all. "Our Friends" included the Argentines he'd just left, Victoria Ocampo, Borges, the French exile Roger Caillois, but also the greater public, no one of them immune. He wrote to them about the two planes, call them plateaus, on which history is made, one composed of episodes in brutal succession and another formed from profound, continuous realities, that one a plane of surface movements and subterranean, unshakeable conditions. There were no synonyms on hand for those.[97]

Back in New Haven that October Focillon confronted the matter of his annual lecture series and chose, for the occasion, to speak of the Revolution of 1848. He divided the topic into four:

Forty-eight: an epoch, an art
Romanticism and realism: Courbet
The Man of the Fields: Millet
Epic Caricature: Daumier.

He explained to the *Yale Daily News* that the nineteenth century was a "preformation of the future." He took the twentieth century to be a "necessary crisis," actually less modern than the nineteenth.[98] He'd made a similar point when speaking in 1934 in Venice during the Art and Reality Conversation sponsored by the Institute for Intellectual Cooperation: "the nineteenth century belongs in actuality to our efforts."[99]

In New York in December at Carnegie Hall, he gave a speech on the Universal Function of France in which he spoke of the French cause in extranational terms, ones stemming from the Declaration of the Rights of Man, terms that built from the utopian thinking of Saint-Simon as well, a function exactly opposed to imperialism, a function that had no use for racial philosophies. The ideas were already present in his speeches from the thirties at the meetings of the Institute. The most beautiful French word, he remarked, was *lumineux*—luminous.[100]

Kubler's lighthouse picked up these signals twenty years after the fact in the way that he could—a new present was again interfering though light and dark remained distinct enough. Knowing this, the light in Kubler's writing shines plainly, without any reason or rhyme, and his laments are no pose:

> ...Why should actuality forever escape our grasp? The universe has a finite velocity which limits not only the spread of its events, but also the speed of our perceptions. The moment of actuality slips too fast by the slow, coarse net of our senses. The galaxy whose light I see now may have ceased to exist millennia ago, and by the same token men cannot fully sense any event until after it has happened, until it is history, until it is the dust and ash of that cosmic storm which we call the present, and which perpetually rages throughout creation.[101]

As for Focillon, when this *actualité* embedded in movements of time pulled ideas into new position, he gave the word more political work to do. The word did not dominate, as the times did not need any special emphasis, but when in March of 1942, he wrote a long speech meant to inaugurate the newly constituted Ecole Libre des Hautes Etudes in New York, he used *actualité* to convene an entire culture, science included. Seen from these prospects, knowledge could not be understood as a formal logic, for research continually brought about a transformation in method, research was spirit, he explained, and so the compelling doubts about the givens of truth that mobilized the *savant* were also the same as those motivating the artist.[102] He had been chosen president of the Ecole Libre, where Claude Lévi-Strauss, the philosopher of science Alexandre Koyré, the sociologist Georges Gurvitch, the Thomist Jacques Maritain, and the linguist Roman Jakobson, among others, were now based, but his health had begun its descent and prevented him from doing much more.[103]

Many of the ideas from that speech would be gathered into his long meditation, a testament, "La Démocratie et la Vague du Passé [Democracy and the Wave of the Past]." He began with the Enlightenment and the series of French revolutions that had broadened into the establishment of successive republics. The horizon now stretching into the future still kept this perspective, he felt, for the world entire. Everything hinged on the choice between tyranny and democracy. At one point he broke to quote from *Les Misérables*, when in the dark of night a watchman calls out, "*Qui vive?*" "Who goes there?" and a disembodied answer comes back, "*La Révolution Française.*"[104] For him it was not theater. The last lines in his meditation speak of shadows darkening the way forward and of the need to erect an image of man at every point on the distant horizon. He died in March 1943, months before there was any real hope of an Allied victory.

In his art history during these same years Focillon had continued to focus on things medieval and had bent himself to a book focussed down on the year 1000, the year medieval Christians thought would bring them the Apocalypse. He left the book unfinished. In its introduction he was opening up a reflection on the study of time and on the diversity in the historical process, not a simple current, not a Hegelian becoming. The historian needed first to find a point on which to construct an observatory, but the observatory itself, he decided, had to contain in its very structure unequal combinations of motion so that from the tower one might be able to discern all the wealth in the topologies of the perspectives. Elsewhere in the book Focillon remarked that history is composed of a three-fold cluster of activating forces—traditions, influences and experiments: "Experiments, one might say," he wrote pragmatically, "dig into the future." Actuality, one might conclude, was their tipping point.[105]

Kubler's lighthouse contains something of the old observatory, though it does not look up, only out. Twenty years later his own *actualité* kept the pulse of Focillon's question. But Kubler's view pulled foregrounds up:

> In my own present, a thousand concerns of active business lie unattended while I write these words. The instant admits only one action while the rest of possibility lies unrealized. Actuality is the eye of the storm: it is a diamond with an infinitesimal perforation through which the ingots and billets of present possibility are drawn into past events. The emptiness of actuality can be estimated by the possibilities that fail to attain realization in any instant: only when they are few can actuality seem full.[106]

Light only shone intermittantly there. Later in *The Shape of Time*, Kubler made the point again about starlight being ancient and compared the stars to art, also old light by the time it reaches our eyes.[107] But art reaches us in things, not language, he observed, which for him put the study of art history somewhere between linguistics and general history.[108] Any lack of splendid isolation did not disturb him. He managed to find the language for what he found. He too drew back from absolute formality; as he considered the effects of series, he too was saying ‹‹and...and...and››. He compared artists to miners working in abandoned shafts down in the dark, following a vein and hoping for a strike.[109] He himself was trying to follow the beam that pierced the diamond. No art historian has ever gone closer to Borges' "Circular Ruins." Kubler only went that way once.

In the fall of 1973 *Artforum* asked Kubler to revisit *The Shape of Time* in light of the present day. He noted that the present day was marked by a transformation in which everything had come to exist in the domain of sensibility, the place where sensations find hierarchy: "everything has come to be intelligible as esthetic experience. ...If you are looking for a cause, it might be in the collapse of restrictions such as taste; the collapse of propriety; the collapse of property. All experience opens up with the collapse of these boundaries between good and bad taste, upper class and lower class, working class and artist class. Experience is opened up to esthetic sensibility by the collapse of a boundary rather than by the creation of a new attitude."[110] On the facing page there was a citation from *The Shape of Time* about the dust and ash of the present.

Toward the end of the interview Kubler said, "Art is everything. All reality is part of the mandate." His interviewer pressed him to go further and expand upon the present again. "Yes," replied Kubler, "it must open up as widely as possible to see the esthetic possibilities of other domains, possibilities for speculation on works of art that had hitherto been invisible elsewhere."[111] So went the seeds that Focillon had sown. The possibilities for speculation in an art history involving facts and objects subject to change would now require the invention of research designs using entirely different levels of inquiry; they would need motivating questions capable of reaching broadly, of finding problems that required more than one person to consider them.

New York

The pace of inquiry, no matter what field, is uneven. In the mid-1930s there was palpable excitement as modern art history took its first steps in a rush; sophisticated ideas were brought to help crack the mysteries of the modern image writ large, including works of art but not excluding words, literature, photographs, cinema and design. Sometimes the ideas were coming through conversation, sometimes they propelled speeches. André Malraux was aware of Walter Benjamin's new essay on the work of art in the age of mechanical reproduction, admired it and cited it when he gave a speech to the Congress of Writers in London in 1936.[112] Or ideas simply coincided. The Europeans might not have read Dewey's new book immediately. Not many knew about the content of Ludwig Wittgenstein's lectures in Cambridge. Many ideas sped alongside one another undetected. They were being driven on by a general effort to catch up with truth. And by the sense that thought had to become more than the thought of thought.

Something comparable happened again in the late 1960s. This time the run of ideas filled the now-established thoughts of modern art with rough, alien tremors; a proper response seemed to require another order of criticism or better, another order of writing. In the United States, Greenberg's idealism was challenged and outflanked on many fronts. Leo Steinberg would lay out "Other Criteria," Lucy Lippard began to log the events that became the calendar of *Six Years: the Dematerialization of the Art Object*.[113] Artists themselves wrote at length. Facts, objects and events washed into a host of foregrounds. They gave onto perspectives of floodplains. For modern art history it was the early work of Meyer Schapiro that provided the points from which new research could proceed. The problems adumbrated in Schapiro's "Nature of Abstract Art" and then analyzed in his 1941 article on Courbet and popular imagery showed a younger group of art historians another way to occupy the space between modern painting and the art critic.[114] The second article was easily accessible to them since it had been published in the *Journal of the Warburg and Courtauld Institutes*. The detail was more than instructive.

Thirty years before "Other Criteria," *Six Years* and *Information*, as the war in Europe was breaking out, Schapiro too had turned to contemplate the Revolution of 1848. Schapiro singled out Courbet and examined the response his pictures received when they went before the public, notwithstanding the howls and cartoons. Schapiro took all of it seriously. He separated the public of Paris from the experience of the provinces; he compared the different reactions with the defenses provided by Courbet's critic friends, like Max Buchon, Pierre Dupont and Champfleury. Both the paintings and the criticism were introducing material from outside the hierarchy of the classical genres. Schapiro isolated these forms and terms as he identified them with the popular culture being asserted in the 1840s. It was hardly an elemental or an elementary culture. It summoned the traditions of artisanal labor with its songs, crudities and folklore, traditions then also being invested with the latest scientific procedures of exactitude and observation; it proposed a view of modernity built up from the bottom and looking forward. It was lyric. Schapiro quoted one of Dupont's songs:

> Où marches-tu, gai compagnon?
> Je m'en vais conquérir la terre;
> J'ai remplacé Napoléon,
> Je suis le prolétaire.[115]

The problem of the statement was made specific. The statement was shown to coexist with an imagery that itself spread semantically. Schapiro's research into this imagery took him into the compendia of Salon criticism, into library print rooms and into the historical arcana of the *métiers* that the nineteenth-century antiquarians had compiled. He laid out the way the critics of painting and literature put forward new terms of support, which came to be called realist, and gave their language a perspective and texture that went beyond questions of right and wrong. He explained the political culture of revolution and reaction around 1848 into which all of this mixed and found common cause. He cited Marx's historical assessments of the time and called them brilliant. He dwelt upon the awakening appreciation for the naïveté of children, quoting Baudelaire's wish "to speak of an inevitable, synthetic, infantile barbarism, which often remains visible in a perfect art (Mexican, Egyptian or Ninivite) and which is derived from the need to see things in the large and to consider them especially in the effect of their ensemble."[116] By the time he had accomplished this synthesis of unstable elements, working by example and sample, he had expanded the field in important ways. He wrote as a realist and as an historian. He had set the bar high. This work had enabled him to move laterally outside the frame of the picture, outside the hierarchies of art criticism also, and to show the transient, empirical tang in forms and words, their salt. It took more than one person and another generation to grasp the import of what he had done.

In February 1970 *Artforum* published an essay entitled "City vs. Country: the Rural Image in French Painting." It issued from a lecture first given in April 1968 by Robert Herbert, then teaching at Yale.[117] It is fitting that the first truly public sign of the movement beyond Schapiro's givens would appear in print in a contemporary art magazine. The same winter Kynaston McShine was preparing *Information*. Smithson was on his way to Utah. The work of art too was opening to the outside in ways that would be permanent.

Lawrence Weiner's "RESIDUE OF A FLARE IGNITED UPON A BOUNDARY" could be seen on nearby pages in that February *Artforum*. Weiner's work had existed as a statement first, with the proviso that it might, like his other statements, be built. In the event, it came to be—an Army surplus flare brought from the States, flashing red-orange and yellow fire, briefly, over land and sea before puddling out on the city limits of Amsterdam. "RESIDUE" became reality for the sake of the exhibition *Op Losse Schroeven* [*Square Pegs in Round Holes,* more literally, *On Loose Screws*].[118] Herbert's essay would be taken to be a harbinger of a new social history of art.

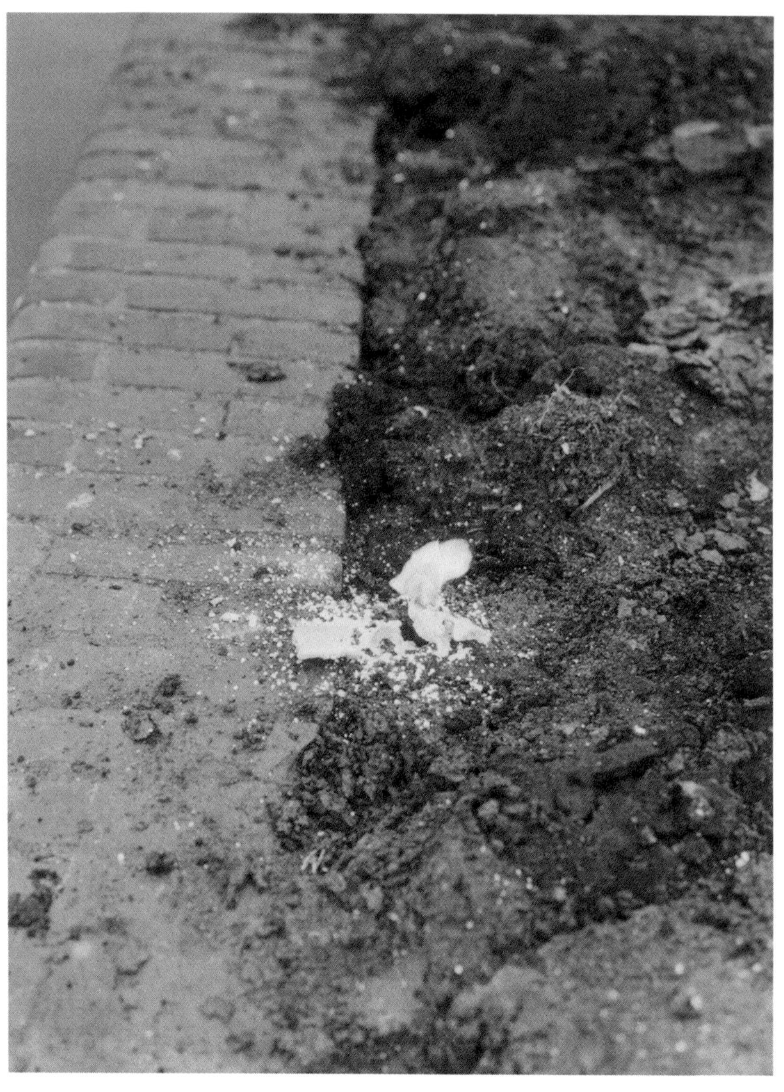

Lawrence Weiner, *THE RESIDUE OF A FLARE IGNITED UPON A BOUNDARY*. Performance, Amsterdam, 1969.

The work of art had already been open to the outside, if one could see beyond the prejudices. That was the point of the new social history of art that bore down on the nineteenth century. It would trigger a new expansion in modern art history at the level of research design and technique. This enabled the art historian not only to see more and to see in masses; but also to take stock of the circling dynamic that knit the seen to the unseen. Implicit was another round in the critique of formalism, a follow-up to the kind that Schapiro had proposed in a letter to Focillon in 1936 when he wrote: "...I believe that unless the peculiar assumptions underlying modern formalism are laid bare, its application to past art will involve various distortions, even in formal analysis (cf. the neglect of undrawn elements, like the glance, in formal analyses of past art.)"[119] Echoes of these ideas were perceptible. Art did not need to be bound or defined solely by media, or a single order of sensation. There were other ways to pose questions, to test boundaries, to look. Herbert had been in contact with Schapiro since 1953, while he was still in graduate school.

Herbert began his *Artforum* essay by sketching the large historical forces of urban-industrial revolution unfolding in the mid-nineteenth century. They were not always evident in the first paintings of modern life. But the city, though unseen, was never altogether absent from any picture of the country; the provinces had been equally affected by these forces, mainly via the ensuing depopulation; Paris had doubled in size in the twenty years between 1831 and 1851. Herbert's essay proceeded to mine demographic evidence. He used it to push through the unseen and undrawn, the latent and the indirect, to an analysis of the painting of landscape and heavy labor. Yet when Herbert deployed demographics to map the path of an historical force, he took care to suspend this material in his argument; the power in the material was not bent; it was not destined to become part of a painting, it remained intact, remained the kind of knowledge that one could only view from the outside and scrutinize, the kind of knowledge that would not flatten into veneer. Historical material was entering art history and opening up questions in a demonstrably different way. Relations between things and pictures became more complex. That historical material sat side by side with the work being done by artists, demanding equal attention, made for an art history that seemed to open floodgates. Whether a modern past or present, it hardly mattered.

Herbert set up a dialectic between the country and the city in mid-century France and proceeded to complicate it. Artists like Delacroix were cited speaking about other things besides art. The political views presented were diverse. Good communication was not guaranteed. Modern painting was arising out of a fundamental instability, to be observed and constructed from the Old Master tradition; the painters were transforming the inherited genres and figures as they shaded and scumbled the silhouettes of sowers and gleaners and harvesters. Change combined with continuity. Herbert worked on this problem by sample, empirically. The paintings of Millet were put front and center. Critics actually saw Michelangelo's energy as well as the rustic proletarian in Millet's *Sower*; those who knew the steep hillsides around Cherbourg could recognize them in Millet's slopes. Herbert laid out these shifting, material points in much the same way that the mid-nineteenth-century painters had. He did so while emphasizing the labor of the painter.

All labor is not equal or the same. This was an art history that examined the social relations that moved inside and outside mid-nineteenth-century painting and then proceeded to put it into relation to the twentieth-century present. For this modern idyll, replete with layers of relations and outright dialectic, had been afterward handed down, taken to the suburbs or given over to anarchism, portending a modern tradition. Herbert spent time discussing the way Van Gogh came to consider his pigments to be clay, a return to the earth he was painting and to the techniques he too had inherited. Van Gogh had especially admired Millet, the man who had written, "Art is not a picnic. It is a combat, a set of gears which grinds one up... I am not a philosopher, I do not want to suppress pain, nor find a formula which would render me stoical and indifferent. Pain is perhaps that which makes an artist express himself most forcibly."[120] In the twentieth century, Herbert explained, sculpture from black Africa, "partly because it was misunderstood and thought to be the result of spontaeous outbusts of emotion, entered modern art as the ultimate counter-image of industrial man."[121] It was time to understand. He did not mention the trial of the Black Panthers currently underway in New Haven, nor his family connection to the Berkeley Free Speech movement.

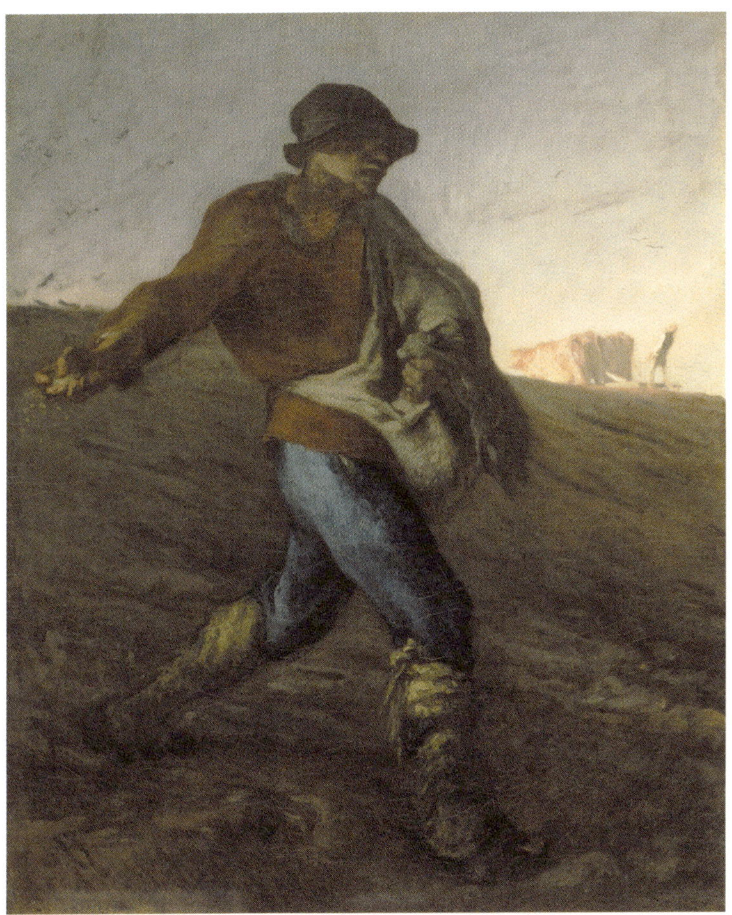

J.-F. Millet, *The Sower*, 1850. Museum of Fine Arts, Boston.

For a decade already Herbert and his wife, the historian Eugenia W. Herbert, had been organizing the George Orwell Forum for radical Yale graduate and undergraduate students. In 1960 the two of them had published the letters between Pissarro, Signac and other late nineteenth-century anarchists in one of the most respected of the British scholarly journals, *The Burlington Magazine*. At one point the article in the *Burlington* spelled out the reason for their choice:

> With the passing of half a century, we can today appreciate the unique position of the Neo-Impressionists and their friends, and its relevance to our own era. They lived in a period which saw the formation of new

> social and labour movements, a period in which the "social question" was forcing older concerns into the background and imposing itself upon the attentions of all levels of society. ...The central issue was no longer monarchism or despotism versus republicanism, and therefore they did not, like Lamartine or Hugo, think primarily in political terms. They worked for social and economic change. Constitutional reforms and political democracy left them sceptical. Their goal was a society resting on an egalitarian base, an ideal that would have frightened most of the radicals of the Romantic period whose motto had been "liberty and fraternity" rather than the dangerous 'equality.'[122]

They noted that these painters did not paint their politics literally into the motifs they chose. They considered the artists' rejection of urban-industrial subjects to be significant, at once tragic and glorious: "because it represents a consistent and heroic fight against materialism, tawdriness, and facile acceptance of observable reality."[123] Privately Herbert called himself an independent socialist. He wrote in the third person. He asked the past to speak as directly as possible to the future.

Ten years later, in 1970, when he finished "City vs. Country," Herbert raised the problem of his own present differently. He noted the rise, since Marx's day, of revolutions in peasant societies (Russia, China, Egypt, Cuba were his examples), hoping to leap over the intermediate stages of industrialization. They too remain devoted to the image of the peasantry, though not every image of a peasant or farm worker expressed a view to the left (he pointed to *American Gothic*.) "The power of the peasant image to modern man," Herbert concluded, "is shown in the fact that Vincent Van Gogh is the most universally known painter on all continents of the earth. To that extent his art is a contemporary phenomenon, entering into the construction of the popular image of the world, which is an agonized one."[124]

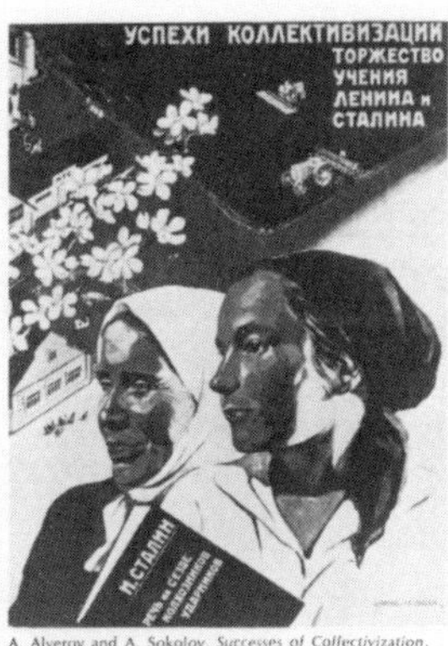

A. Alverov and A. Sokolov, *Successes of Collectivization*, poster, 1934.

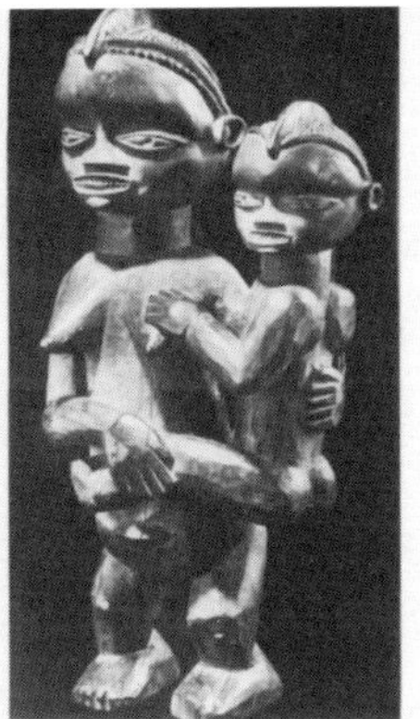

Mbala *Mother and Child*, wood, 17" high. (C. P. Meulendijk, Rotterdam.)

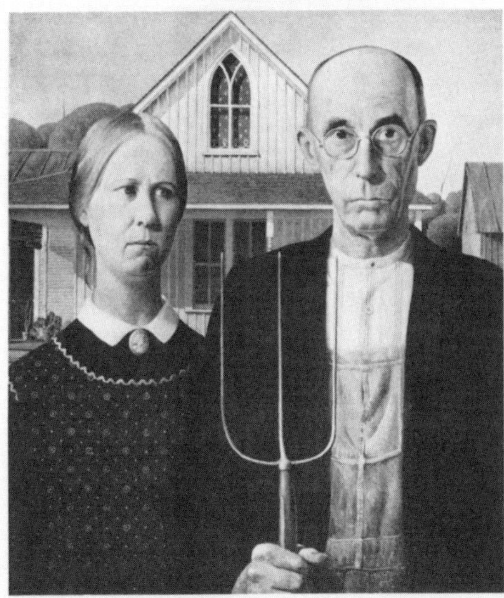

Grant Wood, *American Gothic*, 1930. (Art Institute of Chicago.)

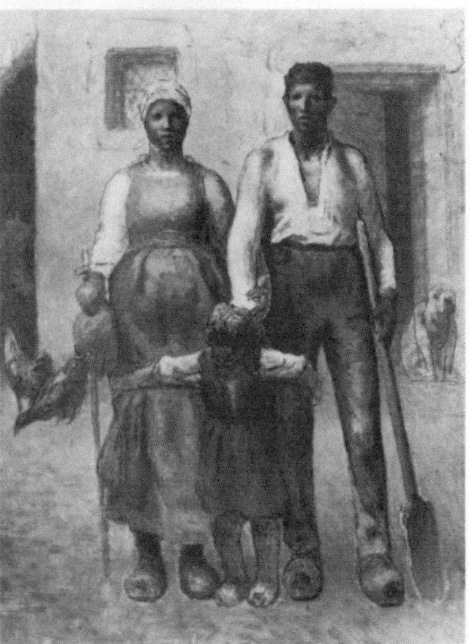

J. F. Millet, *The Peasant Family*, o/c, 43½ x 31¾", unfinished. (National Museum of Wales.)

Robert L. Herbert, "City vs. Country: the Rural Image in French Painting," *Artforum* (February 1970) p. 54.

London

During these same years, in Britain, T. J. Clark returned to the Courbet problems Schapiro had raised and reopened the real space between the painting and the critic, wide, adding more voices. He had had the benefit of the work published on the social history and aesthetics of the English working class by E. P. Thompson and Raymond Williams, not to mention the volumes on the social history of art written by Arnold Hauser, but Schapiro's work was giving him his specific point of entry.[125] Clark asked the question about the political value of a person's statements in much more detail. The first stage of this work was published in *The Burlington Magazine* in 1969.[126] Clark was sending a message first to the academy.

Clark's essay began by asking about the place of active politics in Courbet's art. He introduced new evidence, a document, a full-throated announcement actually, written by Max Buchon for an exhibition of Courbet's *Stonebreakers* in Besançon and Dijon in the spring and summer of 1850. The document allowed Clark to see art criticism not as a final judgment but as a piece of evidence to be compared and measured against other pieces, precisely, read closely; the textual field that opened up between the painting and the critic then acquired added dimensions of time, place and ideology. His research cut deep and wide into the archival sources and mobilized hitherto unsuspected detail from police archives, provincial newspapers and the most recent historical work. Words themselves began to compose the stuff of actuality. But they were also being taken to be part of the material sphere of the things they were trying to describe.

Pictorial narratives were separated from the verbal ones; city experience was cut apart from provincial life. Courbet had, after all, retreated to his home town of Ornans in 1849. He was working on the representation of his own class identity in 1850, Clark's argument went, and that meant defining the bourgeois living in the counterpoint of the countryside. He focussed on Courbet's *Burial at Ornans* in

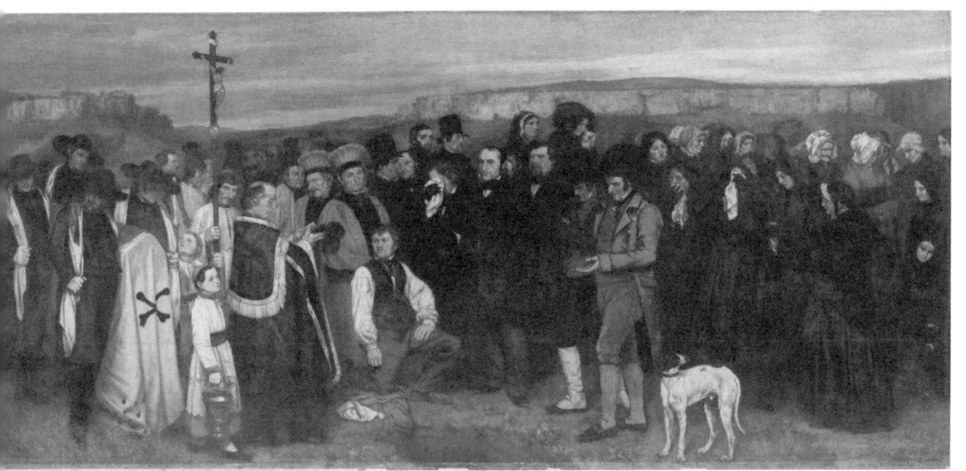

Gustave Courbet, *A Burial at Ornans*, 1849-1850. Musée d'Orsay, Paris.

order to make his ideas clear. At the same time he was obliged, by virtue of the angle of the cuts he had made into these problems, to revise the arguments of Schapiro. Benefitting from the new social histories of France and the *opus* on Flaubert that Sartre was just bringing out, Clark put the artist's own experience of family together with the social order that had arrived to grieve. All of this had been painted into the *Burial*. The painting could not therefore act as a natural history of the event, nor did the community absorb its various individual characters, as Schapiro had proposed. The image and the painted ground of the *Burial* were at pictorial odds with one another, Clark thought, and to press the point he settled into a discussion of Courbet's viscous, expansive blacks, an absolute that defined itself against the lit shapes floating within. This light beyond the pale of color gave concrete shape, he wrote, to terror.

This was the analysis set against the details and effects registered by Courbet's first critics in 1850 and 1851. Art criticism itself was made historical, asked to speak not only for an individual's response but for the different sides of the public response as well. This let Clark unfold his general questions into the maze of particulars: they were questions about the role of political material and about the nature of the public arena into which all of this had spilled. Courbet had understood that the public was not a monolith, that it was split. And in his mind, there was one public to address and another to antagonize. Clark was well aware that publics too had histories and preexistences, but he left out his own experience with the Internationale Situationiste and the political earthquakes still being felt after May 1968. Soon he would be incorporating the semiotic advances of Roland Barthes overtly and they would give his work still another structure.

When Clark rewrote his Courbet material into the book *Image of the People*, published in 1973, he prefaced it with a position paper entitled "On the Social History of Art."[127] It caught fire, like a manifesto. Immediately Clark laid out a list of taboos: this social history of art would not see history to be present as a simple (mirror) reflection; it would not see history playing the part of a "background;" it would question the merely intuitive, i.e. ungrounded, analogies between form and content; it would not limit an artist's social place to that of the art community (we would say art world) alone. He returned to the general question of the public and the artist's desire to have his art produce real social effects, like revolution. He spoke about relations but also about the interface of mediation that entered into the engines of these effects, which could and often did stall. He allowed for fantasies. No art, he declared, *quand même*, is hermetic. "On the Social History of Art" was haunted by the question of the use, including the moral use, of modern art. The chapters that followed kept the question of use alive even as it zeroed in on the minute, but blazing details, the once-unsung sources for thoughts:

> a Parisian critic's careless aside, or a friend's advertisement in a Dijon newspaper; a novel by Wey or a greater novel by Balzac, an almanac and a caricature, a bloody image daubed on a tavern wall; the worries of a Prefect or the result of a trial at Lons-le-Saunier; political strife at Salins, political quiet in Ornans; Courbet collecting peasant songs, or Courbet at carnival time, whey-faced and black-suited, acting the part of Pierrot de la Mort.[128]

In this line of examples a pragmatic legacy can be found, much mediated, still chasing. Clark transcribed the sensation of experience, though the term itself would have dissatisfied him.[129] He would prefer the terms of Marx, of semiotics and psycholanalysis, but these would not fundamentally interfere with the material he introduced. Its expansion was the point. As his preface drew to a close, Clark allowed that the growth of contexts and the new density being introduced would produce another order of difficulty for art historians but he offered a lure: "the work itself may appear in curious, unexpected places; and, once disclosed in a new location, the work may never look the same again."[130] He was not speaking only for himself.

Clark and Herbert, and Kubler in a different way, stood on their separate stages and let the past run out ahead of them. They were opening up the language available to use for the consideration of art, and letting history widen the time of actuality. Words, facts, crowds of people, objects of all sorts were surging forward and asking for sustained attention. The relations between them could be diastolic, fluctuating, dramatic, antique and banal. They were not the stuff of static models or logics or strictly philosophical negations. Language now became the fact and the object, the root and the axe. Something to be used.

Poughkeepsie

Now and then in the early seventies, works of art that put forward the question of boundaries were brought onto college campuses. It is worth asking if they too did not function like seminars. It would not be wrong to say that, independently, artists had been stretching their own research designs and procedures. Boundaries expanded up and down; outcomes could not be controlled. For example, Smithson's partially buried woodshed on the Kent State University campus, made during the winter of 1970. Twenty truckloads of earth were piled on until the woodshed's supporting beam began to crack.[131] Not long afterward, in May, the National Guard killed four students at Kent State as they marched in protest against the American invasion of Cambodia. Kent State immediately became a symbol of social protest that would, retroactively, annex the woodshed. For his part, Smithson had already understood that nothing in art could remain isolated, and that art was destined to be subsumed.

In modern art history the topics normally studied in university seminars were challenged and some began to change; there was a different focus on art's nature and purpose. Linda Nochlin, who likewise had taken her bearings from Schapiro's work on Courbet, and would publish a book on Realism in the fall of 1971, asked the question about the absence of great women artists.[132] She had begun teaching a seminar on Women and Art at Vassar College in 1969. During 1970, she worked on the question in Poughkeepsie; it was previewed, veiled, in the April 3, 1970 issue of the *Misc*, the Vassar student newspaper.[133] She was planning an essay, "Why Have There Been No Great Women Artists?" for an anthology of the new thinking on *Women in Sexist Society*. Her essay would also be published in January 1971 in the most successful of the contemporary art magazines, *ARTnews*, where it was illustrated.

Initially the question "Why Have There Been No Great Women Artists?" was bound less to the role of greatness and more to the matter of rights, notably the right to participate in history. The

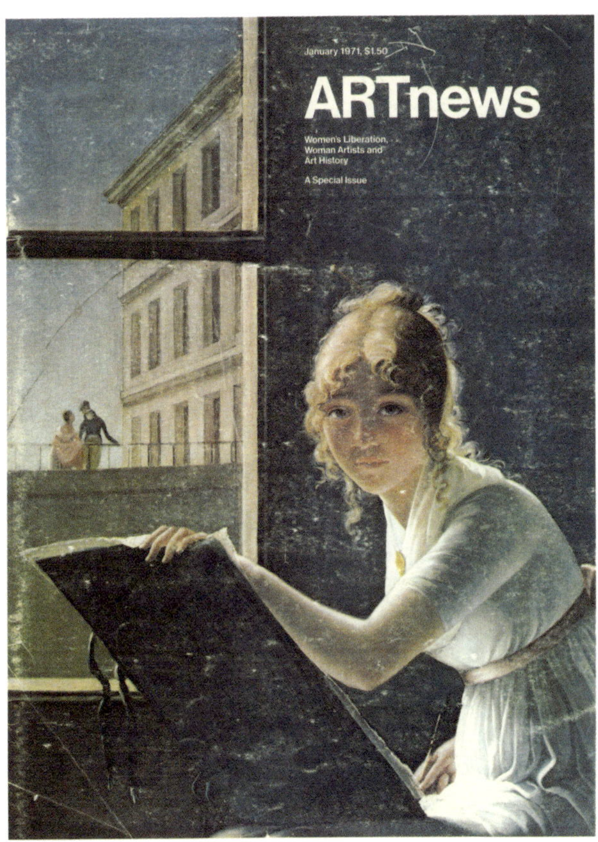

Cover, *ARTnews* (January 1971).

question per se was not new—Malraux made mention of it in *The Voices of Silence*.[134] But Nochlin did more than ask the question, she mobilized and turned it, made it confront the question of education, pointing directly at the age-old differences in women's education to aesthetic form. The question resounded. By 1970 everyone's education to form of all kinds had become an issue. And form itself, aesthetic or not, had become, again, a battleground. The countercultures in the student movement were seeing fit to pose these problems regularly, and aggressively, together with the questions about justice and war and peace and power.

Power does not necessarily come to those who want it. Nochlin's answer to her question was sobering but at the same time energized by the scale she adopted:

The language of art is, more materially, embodied in paint and line on canvas or paper, in stone or clay or plastic or metal–it is neither a sob story nor a confidential whisper.

The fact of the matter is that there have been no supremely great women artists, as far as we know, although there have been many interesting and very good ones who remain insufficiently investigated or appreciated; nor have there been any great Lithuanian jazz pianists, nor Eskimo tennis players, no matter how much we might wish there had been. The fact, dear sisters, is that there are no women equivalents for Michelangelo or Rembrandt, Delacroix or Cézanne, Picasso or Matisse, or even, in very recent times, for de Kooning or Warhol, any more than there are Black American equivalents for the same.

...The fault, dear brothers, lies not in our stars, our hormones, our menstrual cycles, or our empty internal spaces, but in our institutions and our education–education understood to include everything that happens to us from the moment we enter into this world of meaningful symbols, signs, and signals.[135]

In other words, the structure, the shape and the space of one's education matters for all time and space.

The first phase of the question "Why Have There Been No Great Women Artists?" as it circulated in everday student life did not necessarily involve the formal study of the question itself. It lived in conversation; rumors of the Women and Art seminar filtered out. The question came to coexist with the other new questions, new experiences, new events outside the classroom. In this way, the first feminist questions found their footing in paradox. A feminist analysis could be and was taken, using the full force of the paradox, to not-so-specifically feminist questions.

=GORDON MATTA 44 NEW YORK -W-M-150-5'8"- TYPE OT NY PEDLIC
#700298 CHIN SCAR RESUME- THEATER GALLERY EVENTS RECORDED
& UNRECORDED - AGJ, FOOD ART, PMTO-FRY, MUSEUM THE GJBAGE
COLLEGE, GARDENS- PLANS TO PLANT PARKS SOME FLOATING,
OTHERS ON WHEELS THE REST AS SOON AS POSSIBLE STOP TREE
DANCE ON MAY DAY AT VASSAR ORIGINALLY TO BE A SURVIVAL
EXERCISE WANTED A PAYED VACATION IN A TREE. NIPPED IN THE
BUD - A DANCE... THE CLIMBING BODY KEEPS GOING UP ITS
MOVEMENTS CONQUER LIVING SPACE STOP WAITING-WRAPPED-
SUSPENDED- PGH IN CANVAS BAGS CLIMBERS RELAXING IN THE
WIND STOP AND THE SEASONS GO ON DANCE AT THE END OF IT
STRING WILL HOIST ALOFT A GROWTH MODUAL FILLED WITH
MIGRATING WEEDS ANOTHER EXPLOSIVE SPRING BEST=

GORDON:

=(935AE ST)

WU 1201 (R 5-69)

Gordon Matta-Clark, Telegram to Mary Delahoyd for Use as his Artist's Statement in the Catalogue for *26 x 26*, an exhibition at Vassar College, 1971.

May Day 1971. Gordon Matta-Clark had proposed to live for a day in a tree—his contribution to the exhibition *26 x 26* organized by a senior seminar taught by Mary Delahoyd at Vassar. The title of the exhibition was sending a signal of solidarity with the *26 Contemporary Women Artists* on view at the Aldrich Museum in Connecticut that same spring, organized by Lucy Lippard. Lippard limited her list to women who had not yet had a one-person show in New York.[136] The Vassar show put its list of 26 together with no such restriction, and was inviting the work of men. Its catalogue was being modeled on the artists' pages in *Information*.

For his pages in *26 x 26* Gordon Matta-Clark had sent a telegram, a rough statement of purpose. "Originally," he spelled out, "to be a survival exercise wanted a payed [*sic*] vacation in a tree. Nipped in the bud–a dance...The climbing body keeps going up its movements conquer living space. Waiting-wrapped-suspended– pgh[*sic*] in canvas bags climbers relaxing in the wind. And the seasons go on dance at the end of it string will hoist aloft a growth modual[sic] filled with migrating weeds another explosive spring."[137] In the event, a quick thunderstorm broke up this *Tree Dance*.

Into the huge tree that stood before the Chapel, pieces of canvas and nylon made by sailmakers in New York were hung along with the growth module heavy with spore. Nearby was a pod made of transparent parachute material. He had asked Carol Goodden, his new partner, herself a dancer with Trisha Brown, to find him some people for this dance that was not one exactly, meaning it was not to be explicitly choreographed. He wanted dancers of different shapes and sizes to go, two by two, into the pod, peas, mismatched, to live there together for a little while and leave. The light filtering through the pod would reveal them in silhouette. The shadows rested and crawled.[138] Inside came outside, outside went inside. Something was spawning.

The performance itself was unmarked: it had no time frame, no set beginning or end, no audience to speak of. It was an event infiltrated simply by the many shapes of time. The random minds looking up to the tree dance were full of other things, thoughts of the fighting not only in Southeast Asia, but in the Middle East, in Ireland, in Bangladesh, the list was long, and thoughts of impending exams, maybe wondering about the survey of Andy Warhol's work that had opened at the Whitney Museum the night before, maybe tipping back to the Women and Art seminar, maybe tilting toward the summer to come. The minds were full—remembering perhaps the last call for realism at the end of "Why?" Nochlin had taken them all to the watchtower:

> What is important is that women face up to the reality of their history and of their present situation, without

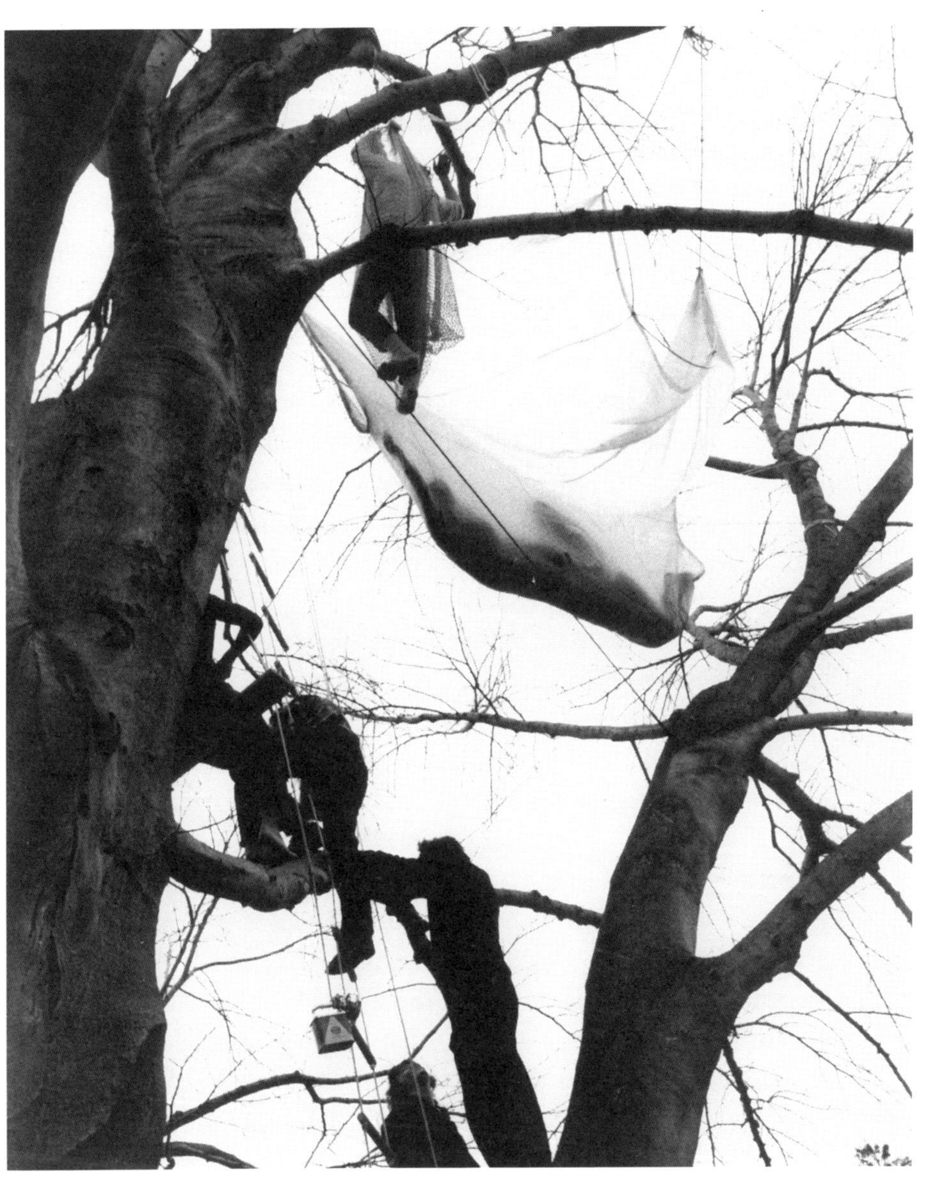

Gordon Matta-Clark, Still from *Tree Dance*, 1971.

making excuses or puffing mediocrity. Disadvantage may indeed be an excuse; it is not, however, an intellectual position. Rather, using as a vantage point their situation as underdogs in the realm of grandeur, and outsiders in that of ideology, women can reveal institutional and intellectual weaknesses in general, and, at the same time that they destroy false consciousness, take part in the creation of institutions in which clear thought-and true greatness-are challenges open to anyone, man or woman, courageous enough to take the necessary risk, the leap into the unknown.[139]

No word stands alone exactly. In March the same minds taking in the spring day had been able to listen to a lecture given in the Chapel by Hannah Arendt. Her topic was "Thinking and Moral Considerations." Arendt wanted to insist upon the vital importance of thinking. Her talk set other explosions in motion. Thinking was vital because thoughtlessness led to evil, to becoming Adolf Eichmanns, she explained. First however she felt it important to define this "*thinking*," especially given the rampant talk of the death of metaphysics. She put paid to that—what they were all witnessing, she explained, was the collapse of the distinction between the sensual and the supersensual. The tree-watchers could remember this lost distinction as the climbers hung and swayed in the sky. Philosophy is in reality a memory—and a perpetual argument.

None of this, Arendt had continued, would affect the basic need to think. It is something to be demanded from every sane person, complete with the warning that thinking is never finished, over and done with. She then pointed to all the difficulty—the way thinking necessarily interrupts one's other activities, requires withdrawal and the endlessness, the way thinking ravels and unravels, like Penelope's veil. She conjured with Socrates to make her points sharpen:

The Athenians told him that thinking was subversive, that the wind of thought was a hurricane which sweeps away all the established signs by which men orient themselves in the world. It brings disorder into the cities and it confuses the citizens, especially the young ones. And though Socrates denied that thinking corrupts, he did not pretend that it improves...[140]

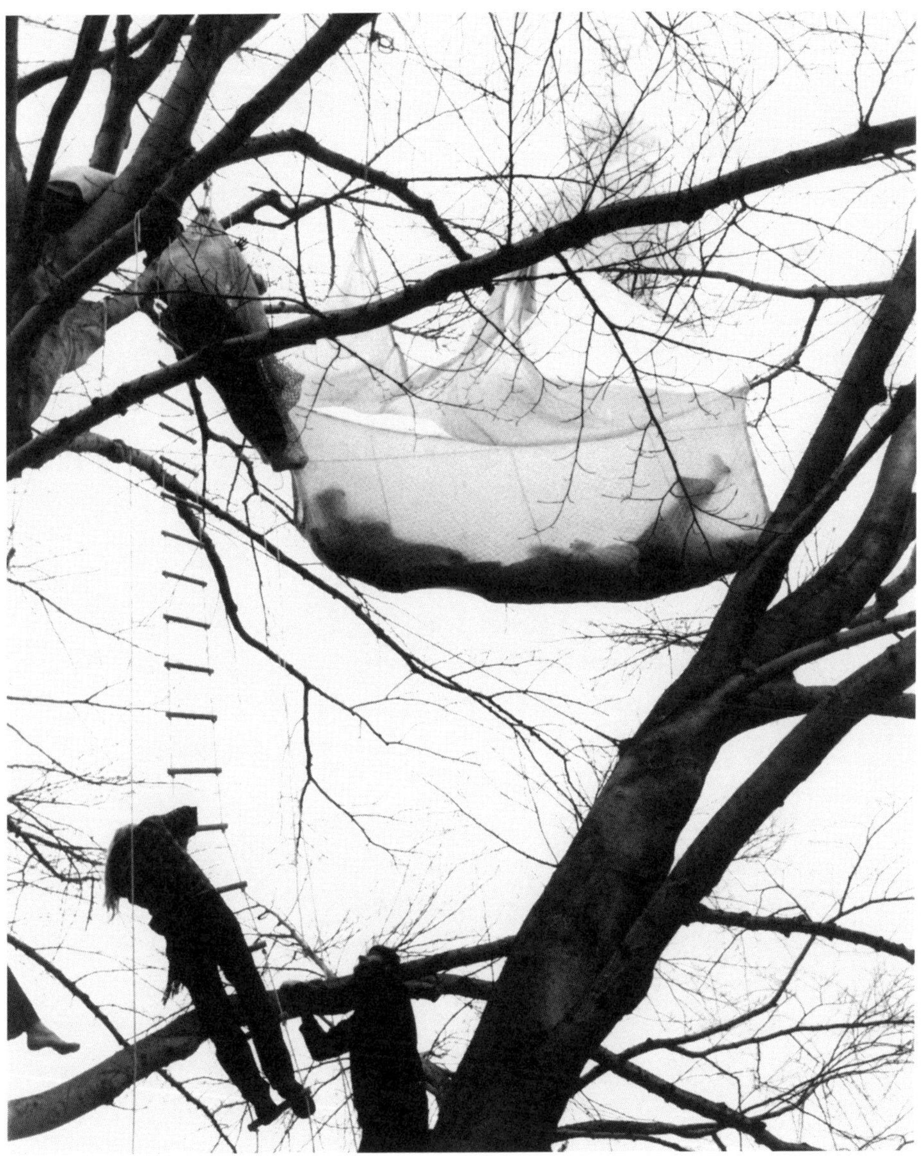

Gordon Matta-Clark, Still from *Tree Dance*, 1971.

All this she told them. She ended with a charge:

> For the thinking ego and its experience, conscience, which "fills a man full of obstacles," is a side effect. And it remains a marginal affair for society at large except in emergencies. For thinking as such does society

little good, much less than the thirst for knowledge in which it is used as an instrument for other purposes. It does not create values, it will not find out, once and for all, what "the good" is, and it does not confirm but rather dissolves accepted rules of conduct. Its political and moral significance comes out only in those rare moments in history when

> Things fall apart; the centre cannot hold;
> Mere anarchy is loosed upon the world,

when

> The best lack all conviction, while the worst
> Are full of passionate intensity.

She was letting the voice of Yeats interrupt, the lines from his "Second Coming," ringing out. She expected everyone there to recognize them. Then she continued her argument without breaking stride.

At these moments, thinking ceases to be a marginal affair in political matters. When everybody is swept away unthinkingly by what everybody else does and believes in, those who think are drawn out of hiding because their refusal to join is conspicuous and thereby becomes a kind of action. The purging element in thinking, Socrates' midwifery, that brings out the implications of unexamined opinions and thereby destroys them–values, doctrines, theories, and even convictions–is political by implication. For this destruction has a liberating effect on another human faculty, the faculty of judgment, which one may call, with some justification, the most political of man's mental abilities. It is the faculty to judge *particulars* without subsuming them under the general rules which can be taught and learned until they grow into habits that can be replaced by other habits and rules.

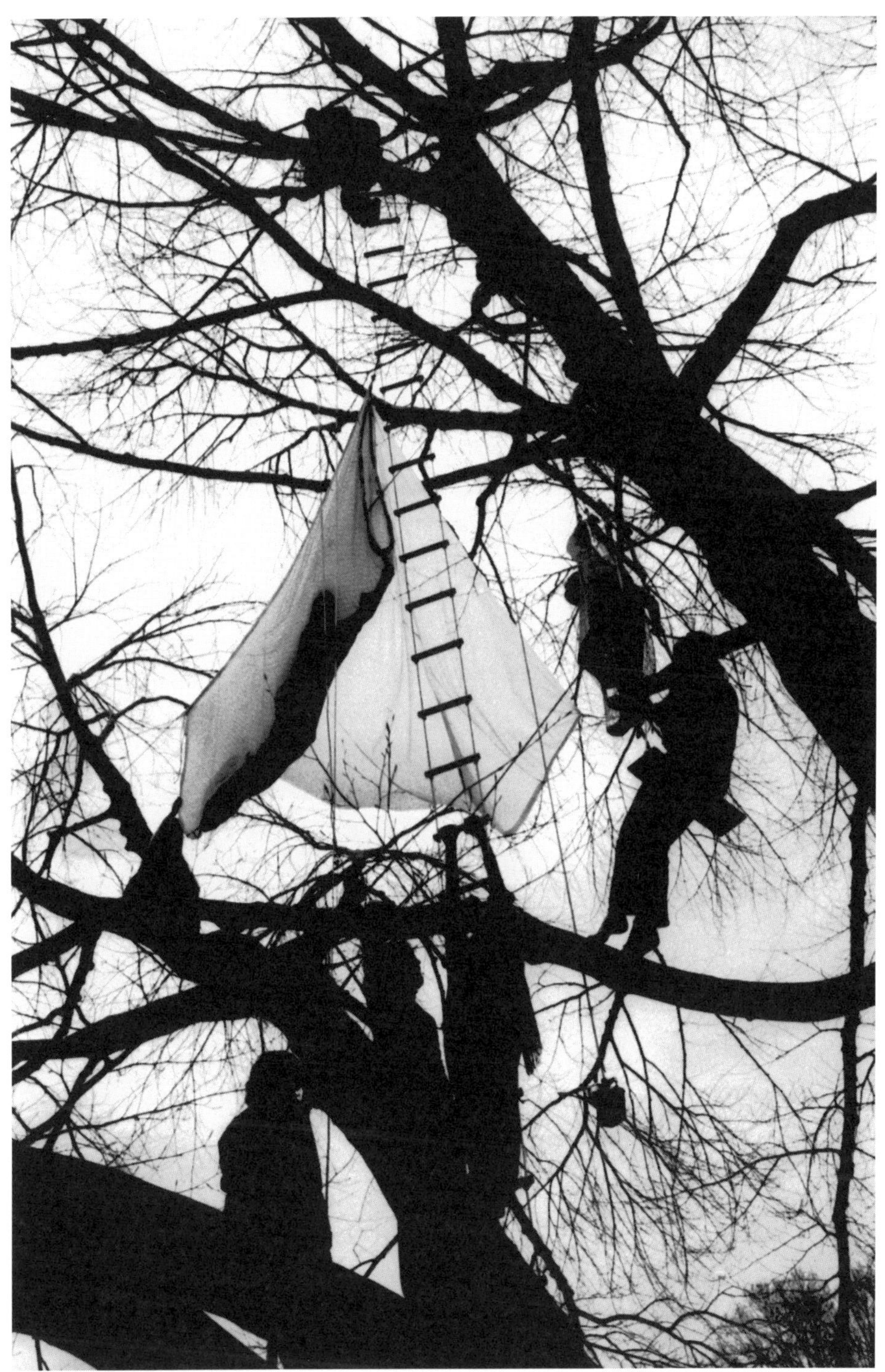

Gordon Matta-Clark, Still from *Tree Dance*, 1971.

As Arendt went on, she took up the charge of the pragmatists, also without saying so, and directed the current ahead:

> The faculty of judging particulars (as Kant discovered it), the ability to say, "this is wrong," "this is beautiful," etc., is not the same as the faculty of thinking. Thinking deals with invisibles, with representations of things that are absent; judging always concerns particulars and things close at hand. But the two are interrelated in a way similar to the way consciousness and conscience are interconnected. If thinking, the two-in-one of the soundless dialogue, actualizes the difference within our identity as given in consciousness and thereby results in conscience as its byproduct, then judging, the by-product of the liberating effect of thinking, realizes thinking, makes it manifest in the world of appearances, where I am never alone and always much too busy to be able to think. The manifestation of the wind of thought is no knowledge; it is the ability to tell right from wrong, beautiful from ugly. And this indeed may prevent catastrophes, at least for myself, in the rare moments when the chips are down.[141]

Thinking and moral considerations were incongruous but they fell together when things fell apart; they hinged on the particular points, the things seen. The questions before her, it became clear, were not general, but as specific as the feet, the ropes, the thunderstorm that will come to interrupt the dance, the leaves, the memory of her words. What if there were no limits to aesthetics?

Philosophy has its real time, just as art has its. Sometimes the two coincide and confront one another. Usually when this happens art and philosophy are asked to match. But there are then the other exceptional times, and this is one of them, when philosophy is *not* a match for art, or vice versa, because neither is a match for history itself. The *Tree Dance* was an event infiltrated by other events: the weekend beforehand 500,000 people had marched on Washington to protest the Vietnam War; students were occupying the administration offices in Vassar's Main Building; in June the *New York Times* would publish the Pentagon Papers detailing the secret history of the American buildup in Vietnam. On May 31st, the *Times* would quote a letter from Gordon Matta-Clark urging an artist boycott of the São Paolo Bienal because "it is now common knowledge that freedom of speech survives nowhere in Brazil."[142]

Tree Dance went upward, against the sky, to the beat of the wind and everything else, another open sight. All that remains of it is a silent film and a few images folded lightly into a few minds. Call them a public too.

At this point, literally, the thoughts that have gone into this book begin.

Notes

1 William James, "Philosophical Conceptions and Practical Results," an address given at the University of California, Berkeley in August 1898 and published in the *University Chronicle*, v. I (September 1898), p. 291. Charles Peirce wrote his own account of pragmatism's beginnings in "A Neglected Argument for the Reality of God," in 1908 for the *Hibbert Journal*, reprinted in *Charles S. Peirce: Selected Writings (Values in a Universe of Chance)*, edited by Philip P. Wiener (New York: Doubleday, 1958), pp. 358–379. Recently all this has been re-ignited by Louis Menand in *The Metaphysical Club: a Story of Ideas in America* (New York: Farrar, Straus and Giroux, 2001), preceded by his anthology *Pragmatism: a Reader* (New York: Vintage, 1997), and before that by Cornel West, *The American Evasion of Philosophy: a Genealogy of Pragmatism* (Madison: University of Wisconsin Press, 1989). Architects have been inspired by John Rajchman, "A New Pragmatism?" from *Anyhow*, edited by Cynthia Davidson (Cambridge: MIT Press, 1998), pp. 212–217. See also the conference at the Buell Center for the Study of American Architecture, Columbia University in May 2000, organized by Rajchman and Joan Ockman, *The Pragmatist Imagination: Thinking About "Things in the Making,"* the proceedings of which were published under that title the same year by Princeton Architectural Press. The conference would have a second iteration at the Museum of Modern Art in New York in November 2000.

2 William James, "What Pragmatism Means," in *Pragmatism: A New Name for Some Old Ways of Thinking, together with four related essays selected from The Meaning of Truth* (New York: Longmans, Green and Company, 1946), pp. 53–55.

3 Citation from "How to Make Our Ideas Clear" as reprinted in *Selected Writings*, p. 117. Both essays appeared originally as follows: "The Fixation of Belief," *Popular Science Monthly* (November 1877), pp. 1–15, and in French as "Comment se fixe la croyance," *Revue Philosophique de la France et de l'étranger*, t. 6 (Décembre 1878), pp. 553–569; "How to Make Our Ideas Clear," *Popular Science Monthly* (January 1878), pp. 286–302 and in French as "Comment rendre nos idées claires," *Revue Philosophique de la France et de l'étranger*, t. 7 (Janvier 1879), pp. 39–57.

4 Thomas Gray, "Elegy Written in a Country Churchyard," *The Oxford Book of English Verse 1250–1900*, edited by Arthur Quiller-Couch (Oxford: Clarendon Press, 1923), p. 518.

5 Peirce, "What Pragmatism Is," originally in *The Monist* (April 1905), reprinted in *Selected Writings*, p. 194.

6 Peirce, "Issues of Pragmatism," in *The Monist* (October 1905), reprinted in *Selected Papers*, p. 221.

7 John Dewey, "The Need for a Recovery of Philosophy," in *Creative Intelligence: essays in the pragmatic attitude* (New York: Henry Holt and Company, 1917), p. 59. On living forward, see p. 12. On Dewey, see Sidney Hook, *John Dewey: an Intellectual Portrait* (New York: John Day Company, 1939) and Jay Martin, *The Education of John Dewey: a Biography* (New York: Columbia University Press, 2002).

8 John Dewey, *Experience and Nature* (Chicago: Open Court Publishing Company, 1925), p. 392. The book would have a second edition in 1929, the revisions coming in the first chapter on Philosophic Method.

9 Dewey, *Art as Experience* (New York: Minton, Balch & Company, 1934).

10 Gilles Deleuze, *Foucault* (Paris: Minuit, 1986), pp. 59, 70, 81. On the use of pragmatism, its new life in Deleuze's philosophy and the nature of the Deleuzian diagram, see John Rajchman's essay, "A New Pragmatism," op. cit. Deleuze himself would say, as an aside in *Qu'est-ce que la philosophie?* (Paris: Minuit, 1991), p. 103, that American pragmatism was then little known in France.

11 Michel Foucault, *Surveiller et punir. Naissance de la prison* (Paris: Gallimard, 1975), p. 206. In English as *Discipline and Punish: the Birth of the Prison*, translated by Alan Sheridan (New York: Random House, 1977).

12 A lecture from the Manet work has survived and been published as Michel Foucault, *La Peinture de Manet*, sous la direction de Maryvonne Saison (Paris: Seuil, 2004).

13 Friedrich Nietzsche, "Attempt at a Self-Criticism," 1886 preface for *The Birth of Tragedy*, in *Basic Writings of Nietzsche*, translated and edited by Walter Kaufmann (New York: Modern Library, 1968), p. 19.

14 Nietzsche, *Ecce homo*, in *Basic Writings*, p. 766.

15 Michel Foucault, *Introduction à l'Anthropologie de Kant*, published together with Foucault's translation of Immanuel Kant, *Anthropologie du point de vue pragmatique* (Paris: Vrin, 2008), p. 33. This was Foucault's *habilitation* thesis, presented in 1961; the translation of Kant was published in late 1964. At the time Foucault withheld the publication of his introduction, which would become the first step to his next project, *The Order of Things*.

16 *The Order of Things: an archaeology of the human sciences* (New York: Random House, 1970), p. ix. First published in French as *Les Mots et les choses* (Paris: Gallimard, 1966).

17 *The Order of Things*, p. ix.

18 Ibid., p. xii.

19 *Surveiller et punir,* p. 35.

20 Deleuze, *Foucault,* p. 124.

21 See especially Foucault, *"Qu'est-ce que les Lumières,"* excerpted from his course at the Collège de France for January 5, 1983 and published in *Dits et écrits,* t. 4, pp. 679–688. In English, along with the rest of the course, in *The Government of Self And Others: Lectures at the Collège de France,* edited by Frédéric Gros, translated by Graham Burchell (New York: Palgrave Macmillan, 2010). Earlier Sylvère Lotringer collected a group of Foucault's meditations on Kant's *Aufklärung* article into an extremely influential book, *The Politics of Truth,* edited by Sylvère Lotringer and Lysa Hochroth (New York: Semiotext(e), 1997).

22 The exchange, recorded March 4, 1972, was translated into English as "Intellectuals and Power" by Donald Bouchard and Sherry Simon in the collection of Foucault's essays, *Language, Counter-memory, Practice,* edited by Donald Bouchard (Ithaca: Cornell University Press, 1977), p. 208.

23 Ibid., p. 90.

24 Paul Klee, *Pedagogical Sketchbook* (a Bauhaus book first published in German in 1925), introduction and translation by Sibyl Moholy-Nagy (London: Faber & Faber, 1953).

25 Deleuze, *Foucault,* p. 129. The quote is unreferenced but it comes from William Faulkner, *The Unvanquished* (New York: Random House, 1938), p. 8.

26 Gilles Deleuze et Félix Guattari, *Mille plateaux* (Paris: Minuit, 1980), e.g., pp. 184, 105, 115.

27 Postface written for the French edition of Melville's *Bartleby* in 1989, reprinted in *Critique et Clinique* (Paris: Minuit, 1993), pp. 89–114.

28 Jean-Paul Sartre, "*La Temporalité chez Faulkner,*" *Situations*, I (Paris: Gallimard, 1947), pp. 66–67.

29 "A propos de John Dos Passos et de ‹‹1919››," op. cit., p. 17. As translated by Annette Michelson in Sartre, *Literary and Philosophical Essays* (New York: Criterion Books, 1955), p. 90. On Marker's early contact with Sartre, see the memoirs of those who had been in *lycée* with him: Simone Signoret, *La Nostalgie n'est plus ce qu'elle était* (Paris: Seuil, 1976), p. 32; Anatole Dauman, *Anatole Dauman. Argos Films. Souvenir-Ecran* (Paris: Centre Georges Pompidou, 1989), pp. 14–15; Bernard Pingaud, *Une Tâche sans fin. Mémoires* (Paris: Seuil, 2009), pp. 92–93.

30 Chris Marker quoted in "Rare Marker," an interview with Samuel Douhaire and Annick Rivoire in *Libération* on March 5, 2003 and translated into English by Marker for the booklet accompanying the Criterion Collection's DVD release of *La Jetée* and *Sans Soleil* in 2007, p. 38.

31 Chris Marker and I had an ongoing conversation about utopia, beginning in 1998. He spoke once or twice about his wartime experience in a Swiss labor camp, and then as a *petit maquisard* (never a parachutist), then joining up with the American army, with Joyce's *Ulysses* as the book he took to tide him through the war. He remembered with pleasure the marvel of the Eames' Moscow installation and volunteered the thought of it sparking something later for *La Jetée*.

32 Gilles Deleuze and Félix Guattari, *Mille plateaux* (Paris: Minuit, 1980), p. 37, my translation. See also Deleuze's interview "Trois Questions sur *Six Fois Deux,*" *Cahiers du Cinéma*, no. 271 (November 1976), pp. 5–12 and, for the context, Antoine de Baecque, *Godard: Biographie* (Paris: Grasset, 2010). After 1968, Godard and Deleuze would meet, according to Godard in "Jean-Luc Godard à Daniel Cohn-Bendit: 'Qu'est-ce qui t'intéresse dans mon film?'" *Télérama* (15 May 2010).

33 Mike Nichols as quoted by John Lahr, "After *Angels*: Tony Kushner's Promethean Itch," *The New Yorker* (January 3, 2005), p. 48: "For the first-rate artist, there is a moment when he's really getting revved up, and the time just flows into him. It only happens once. It happens without his awareness at all. He planned nothing. He was just going ahead doing this next thing."

34 Alfred Barr, Jr., *Cubism and Abstract Art* (New York: MoMA, 1936), p. 13: [Abstract art] is based upon the assumption that a work of art, a painting for example, is worth looking at primarily because it presents a composition or organization of color, line, light and shade. Resemblance to natural objects, while it does not necessarily destroy these esthetic values, may easily adulterate their purity. Therefore, since resemblance to nature is at best superfluous and at worst distracting, it might as well be eliminated. ...Such an attitude of course involves a great impoverishment of painting, an elimination of a wide range of values, such as the connotations of subject matter, sentimental, documentary, political, sexual, religious; the pleasures of easy recognition; and the enjoyment of technical dexterity in the imitation of material forms and surfaces. But in his art the abstract artist prefers impoverishment to adulteration.

35 Meyer Schapiro, "Nature of Abstract Art," *Marxist Quarterly* (January–March 1937), pp. 77–98; reprinted in his collected essays, *Modern Art 19th and 20th centuries. Selected Papers* (New York: Braziller, 1978), pp. 185–211. The topic has received much attention, notably by Thomas Crow: "Modernism and Mass Culture in the Visual Arts," in *Modernism and Modernity: the Vancouver Conference Papers*, edited by Benjamin H. D. Buchloh, Serge Guilbaut and David Solkin (Halifax: Press of the Nova Scotia College of Art and Design, 1983), pp. 224–235, and his chapter on Schapiro in *The Intelligence of Art* (Chapel Hill: University of North Carolina Press, 1999), pp. 1–23. Andrew Hemingway's two essays, "Meyer Schapiro and Marxism in

the 1930s," *Oxford Art Journal*, v. 17 (1994), pp. 13–29 and "Meyer Schapiro: Marxism, Science and Art," in *Marxism and the History of Art: from William Morris to the New Left*, edited by Andrew Hemingway (London: Pluto Press, 2006), pp. 123–142, remain indispensable for their ability to position Schapiro's thinking on the arts and architecture in the American debates, which were hardly provincial. See also Hemingway's book, *Artists on the Left: American Artists and the Communist Movement, 1926–1956* (London: Yale University Press, 2002).

36 Meyer Schapiro, "The Social Bases of Art," *Worldview in Painting—Art and Society: Selected Papers* (New York: Braziller, 1999), p. 123. *Artists Against War and Fascism: Papers of the First American Artists' Congress (1936)*, reprinted and edited by M. Baigell and J. Williams (New Brunswick: Rutgers University Press, 1986), pp. 103–113.

37 Ibid., pp. 127–128.

38 "Nature of Abstract Art," op. cit., p. 86.

39 Ibid., p. 88.

40 Ibid., p. 90.

41 Ibid., p. 97.

42 John Dewey, *Art as Experience* (New York: Minton, Balch & Co., 1934), p. 342.

43 *Art as Experience*, p. 344.

44 Schapiro took Dewey's course, "Philosophy 191: Types of Philosophical Thought," in the winter of 1923. In 1926 he wrote a critical aside about the too elementary ways of seeing advocated by Barnes and by extension Dewey in a letter to his future wife. *Meyer Schapiro Abroad: Letters to Lillian and Travel Notebooks*, edited by

Daniel Esterman (Los Angeles: Getty Research Institute, 2009), p. 107. In the Meyer Schapiro Collection, Rare Book and Manuscript Library, Columbia University, MS#1121, Series IV.3, box 235, f. 38 there are three pages of notes dated 1929/30 on "The sources of pragmatism." In Subseries V.5, box 343, f. 1–2 there are research notes from the thirties on Dewey's work, including the chapters of *Art as Experience* that Dewey had asked him to read while in manuscript.

45 Meyer Schapiro, "Philosophy and Worldview in Painting" (1958–68), *Worldview in Painting*, pp. 71–72. The handwritten notes for this footnote originally formed a talk given at a symposium at New York University on *Art as Experience*, now in the Rare Book and Manuscript Library, Columbia University, Meyer Schapiro Collection, MS #1121, Subseries III, 3.3, box 198, f. 19. See also Schapiro's interview with David Craven, "A Series of Interviews (July 15, 1992–January 22, 1995)," *RES: Anthropology and Aesthetics*, no. 31 (spring 1997), p. 159.

46 *Art as Experience*, pp. 315–20.

47 The picture had not appeared in *Cubism and Abstract Art* but it had figured prominently in the most recent English edition of Elie Faure's *History of Art, v. IV—Modern Art*, translated by Walter Pach (New York: Harper & Brothers, 1924), p. 481.

48 Meyer Schapiro, "The Arts Under Socialism," undated and apparently unpublished essay from 1937, in *Worldview in Painting*, p. 132.

49 Gertrude Stein, *Picasso* (New York: Dover, 1984), p. 12, first edition 1938.

50 Ibid., p. 50.

51 The list appears in a letter to Kenneth Howard, February 5, 1936, Meyer Schapiro Collection, Series II, box 157, f. 2.

52 See the notes remaining for it in the Meyer Schapiro Collection, Subseries IV.4, boxes 241 and 242. Oxford University Press initiated the discussion in 1937, but Phaidon Press and the Museum of Modern Art became involved.

53 The sculpture, √2, was included in the Museum of Modern Art's group exhibition, *Fourteen Americans,* that fall and there Noguchi put the life questions into his statement: "The essence of sculpture is for me the perception of space, the continuum of our existence. ...Since our experiences of space are, however, limited to momentary segments of time, growth must be the core of existence. We are reborn, and so in art as in nature there is growth, by which I mean change attuned to the living. Thus growth can only be new, for awareness is the everchanging adjustment of the human psyche to chaos. If I say that growth is the constant transfusion of human meaning into the encroaching void, then how great is our need today when our knowledge of the universe has filled space with energy, driving us toward a greater chaos and new equilibriums. I say it is the sculptor who orders and animates space, gives it meaning." Dorothy Miller, *Fourteen Americans* (New York: MoMA, 1946), p. 39. See Thomas Hess, "Isamu Noguchi '46," *Art News* (September 1946), pp. 34–38, and 50–51 and the unsigned, "Speaking of Pictures...Japanese-American Sculptor Shows Off Weird New Works," *LIFE* (November 11, 1946), pp. 12–13 and 15. Upon his release from the Poston camp, Noguchi wrote "Trouble Among Japanese Americans," *The New Republic,* v. 108 (February 1, 1943), pp. 142–143. For the context see Robert J. Maeda, "Isamu Noguchi: 5—7—A, Poston, Arizona," in *Last Witnesses: Reflections on the Wartime Internment of Japanese Americans,* edited by Erica Harth (New York: Palgrave Macmillan, 2001), pp. 153–166, and Amy Lyford, "Noguchi, Sculptural Abstraction and the Politics of Japanese American Internment," *Art Bulletin,* v. 85 (March 2003), pp. 137–151.

54 J. L. Borges, "The Circular Ruins," in *View,* series V, no. 6 (January 1946) in Paul Bowles' translation reprinted in *View: Parade*

of the Avant-Garde, 1940–1947, edited by Charles Henri Ford, foreword by Paul Bowles (New York: Thunder's Mouth Press, 1991), p. 191. See this anthology for a complete inventory of the magazine's contents and a sampling from its pages. On Borges, see Emir Rodriguez Monegal, *Jorge Luis Borges: a Literary Biography* (New York: E. P. Dutton, 1978).

55 Sartre lectured on "Nouvelles Tendences du Théâtre Français," in the Carnegie Chamber Music Hall on March 5, 1946. Francis Lee, "A Soldier Visits Picasso," appeared in the March 1946 *View* and is reprinted in *View: Parade of the Avant-Garde*, pp. 222–224.

56 Meyer Schapiro, "On a Painting of Van Gogh," *View*, series VI, no. 5 (October 1946), pp. 8–14. Schapiro's correspondence with Charles Henri Ford, including Parker Tyler's edit for the essay, is now part of the Charles Henri Ford Papers, Beinecke Library, Yale University, YCAL MSS32, box 2, f. 102 and box 5, f. 321. Schapiro kept his side of the correspondence with Ford and Tyler, which begins in 1938. In 1942 he contributed to a questionnaire for *View*, nos. 11–12 asking "`What do you see in the stars?`" He answered: "`Death is the disappearing point of the unconscious. The stars and the unfinished message of the universe.`" The idea for the Van Gogh article is first discussed in the spring of 1946. By July he knew about the Noguchi cover. Meyer Schapiro Collection, Series II, box 127, f. 5. Schapiro's drafts and notes for the article are found in Series II, box 222, f. 8, as is the letter that Rudolph Arnheim wrote him about it, recalling that a print of the picture had been hanging on the wall of Schapiro's office when they had last visited.

57 Ibid., p. 14.

58 Willem de Kooning a few years later gave a short talk about the new postwar ground and those who felt that the light of the atomic bomb would change painting once and for all. De Kooning spoke in parables and so turned to speak of those eyes that had actually seen atomic light: they had melted, he said, out of sheer ecstasy; for one instant, he then remarked, everybody was the same color. Not only

that, he then added, the light had made angels out of everybody. Willem de Kooning, "What Abstract Art Means to Me," a talk written for a Museum of Modern Art Symposium, first published in *The Museum of Modern Art Bulletin*, v. XVIII (spring 1951), reprinted in Thomas Hess, *Willem de Kooning* (New York: Museum of Modern Art, 1968), p. 146.

59 On his meeting with Walter Benjamin, see James Thompson and Susan Raines, "A Vermont Visit with Meyer Schapiro (August 1991)," *Oxford Art Journal*, v. 17 (1994), pp. 7–8.

60 Meyer Schapiro Collection, Series V, box 356, f. 20, "Physicalism and Art." The ongoing work of the Vienna Circle was being published in their magazine *Erkenntnis*. Otto Neurath, "Sociologie im Physicalismus" appeared there in v. 2 (1931), translated into English as "Sociology and Physicalism," in A. J. Ayer, ed., *Logical Positivism* (Glencoe, Illinois: The Free Press, 1959), pp. 282–317.

61 Schapiro's papers are full of notes and correspondence with regard to this essay, which was never written to his own satisfaction and, despite entreaties written as late as 1960, never handed in. See the Meyer Schapiro Collection, Subseries IV.3, box 236, f. 28 for some of the early correspondence and notes. On his effort to set up a meeting with Wittgenstein, see his correspondence with Ernest Nagel, Meyer Schapiro Collection, Series II, box 150, f. 8, letter of June 12, 1939. Nagel himself had failed to meet Wittgenstein during his trip in 1935 but had seen the notes from his lectures; this forms part of his account of the new European logic and its physicalism, published in the *Journal of Philosophy*, v. XXXIII (January 2, 1936), p. 17; on Wittgenstein: "Traditional philosophy, according to him, is a mélange of problems, some of which are genuinely empirical ones and some non-sensical combinations of words due to grammatical confusion. The tendency to generate 'profound' questions not amenable to empirical inquiry–the perennial problems of philosophy–he regards as a disease which it is the task of sound philosophy to cure. The reinstatement of the unsophisticated, untroubled view of

the man in the street is apparently the goal of philosophic activity, though I suspect that Wittgenstein would regard the man cured in his way of the dreaded affliction as somehow better off than the one who has never succumbed to philosophizing in the traditional manner." The point here, Nagel goes on to say, is not to make theory but instead to make specific clarifications. Much of this, he adds, reads like a page from Peirce.

62 "The Investigation and Criticism of the Arts—for Encyc. Unity of Science," Meyer Schapiro Collection, Subseries IV.3, box 236, f. 28. For more on the context see George A. Reisch, *How the Cold War Transformed Philosophy of Science: to the Icy Slopes of Logic* (Cambridge: Cambridge University Press, 2005), p. 66ff.

63 Drafts of letters to Wolfgang Paelen [sic], Meyer Schapiro Collection, Series II, box 157, f. 2. On Schapiro's work during the war see Hemingway, "Meyer Schapiro and Marxism in the 1930s," op. cit., p. 22ff.

64 Jacques Derrida's critique of Schapiro, "The Still Life as a Personal Object—a note on Heidegger and Van Gogh," *The Reach of Mind: Essays in Memory of Kurt Goldstein*, edited by M. G. Simmel (New York: Springer, 1968), pp. 203–209, was complex and took on Martin Heidegger's reading of the painting too. It would be published in first form in *Macula*, no. 3 (1977) along with a French translation of Schapiro's essay. Derrida would give this essay as a lecture at Columbia on October 6, 1977 as part of the Theory of Literature University Seminar organized by Marie-Rose Logan and Edward Said. Schapiro was present in the audience and later recounted the episode to David Craven, saying "I was abrupt with him, because he neither understood nor cared to understand the nature of my criticism." Craven, op. cit., p. 161. Derrida would publish a second version of this work as part of his book, *La Vérité en peinture* (Paris: Flammarion, 1978). Earlier, Schapiro might have called this interpretative work an expression statement. Schapiro would publish his "Further Notes on Heidegger and Van Gogh" made in 1994 in

his fourth volume of collected essays, *Theory and Philosophy of Art: Style, Artist, and Society* (New York: Braziller, 1994), pp. 143–151, without mentioning Derrida at all. His response to Derrida in 1977 has been recorded by David Shapiro in "Van Gogh, Heidegger, Schapiro, Derrida: The Truth in Criticism (Notes on Restless Life)," in *Van Gogh 100*, edited by Joseph Masheck (Westport, Connecticut: Greenwood, 1996), p. 293. Unfortunately no notes seem to have been taken for that particular meeting of the Theory of Literature University Seminar.

65 Alexander Dorner, *The Way Beyond 'Art'—the Work of Herbert Bayer* (New York: Wittenborn, 1947), p. 229.

66 Ibid., p. 219.

67 Alexander Dorner, "Considérations sur la Signification de l'Art Abstrait," *Cahiers d'Art*, nos. 7–8 (1931), pp. 354–357.

68 John Dewey, preface to Alexander Dorner, *The Way Beyond 'Art'*, p. 9.

69 Samuel Cauman would use the term as the title for the biography he wrote with Dorner's approval and help, *The Living Museum: Experiences of an Art Historian and Museum Director—Alexander Dorner* (New York: NYU Press, 1958).

70 Ibid., pp. 118–9.

71 Dorner, *The Way Beyond 'Art,'* p. 232.

72 The idea had been suggested to him by a student at Bennington, Bobbie Goldberg. See Cauman, op. cit., p. 186 and Joan Ockman's important article, "The Road Not Taken: Alexander Dorner's Way Beyond 'Art,'" from *Autonomy and Ideology: Positioning an Avant-Garde in America*, edited by R. E. Somol (New York: Monacelli, 1997), p. 117. In May 2000, Casey Nelson Blake, Joan Ockman and John Rajchman organized a prescient cross-disciplinary conference,

The Pragmatist Imagination, held at the Buell Center for the Study of American Architecture at Columbia University and The Museum of Modern Art in New York.

73 Alfred Barr, Jr., *What is Modern Painting?* (New York: MoMA, 1943), p. 12.

74 Clement Greenberg, "Avant-Garde and Kitsch," *The Collected Essays and Criticism*, edited by John O'Brian, v. 1 (Chicago: University of Chicago Press, 1986), p. 8. The essay first appeared in *Partisan Review* (fall 1939). Greenberg's early thinking takes its cues from many of Dewey's arguments in *Art as Experience*, which Greenberg in the end will fundamentally oppose.

75 John Hightower, "New Directions for the Future," May 7, 1970 proposal for a new capital campaign which was to have been announced in June but was instead delayed. John B. Hightower Papers, I.1.3. The Museum of Modern Art Archives, New York. The ideas appeared already during his interviews for the position and in his first interview for the *New York Times* with Grace Glueck, "Modern Names Hightower Director," *New York Times*, January 9, 1970. Hightower would serve as Director from May 1, 1970 until January 5, 1972.

76 Kynaston McShine, "Essay," *Information*, edited by Kynaston McShine (New York: MoMA, 1970), p. 138. The cover was designed by Marc Ratliff based on pictures supplied by Kynaston McShine, according to their correspondence, now in the Curatorial Exhibition Files, Exh. #934. MoMA Archives, NY.

77 Hélio Oiticica statement in *Information, p. 103.*

78 The catalogue gives a long but partial list of the poets reading their poems, op. cit., p. 137. The checklist for the exhibition can be found in the Registrar Exhibition Files, Exh. #934. MoMA Archives, NY. The Art Workers' Coalition poster used a photograph by Ron Haeberle of the civilians massacred by American soldiers

at My Lai in March 1968. On the Art Workers' Coalition and their interactions with the Museum of Modern Art, see Julia Bryan-Wilson, *Art Workers: Radical Practice in the Vietnam War Era* (Berkeley: University of California Press, 2009).

79 John Hightower, "11 West 53rd Street: from the Director," *The Museum of Modern Art Members Newsletter*, November 1970, p. 1.

80 Robert Smithson, "Quasi-Infinities and the Waning of Space," *Robert Smithson: the Collected Writings*, edited by Jack Flam (Berkeley: University of California Press, 1996), pp. 34–35, first appearing in *Arts Magazine* (November 1966). Pamela Lee has written on Smithson's exchange with Kubler's ideas, as well as those of Norbert Wiener, reading their texts through one another as part of her greater argument in *Chronophobia: On Time in the Art of the 1960s* (Cambridge: MIT Press, 2004), chapter 4 "Ultramoderne: Or, How George Kubler Stole the Time in Sixties Art."

81 Smithson, "The Spiral Jetty," *Robert Smithson: the Collected Writings*, p. 146, first appearing in *Arts of the Environment*, edited by György Kepes (New York: Braziller, 1972).

82 George Kubler, *The Shape of Time: Remarks on the History of Things* (New Haven: Yale University Press, 1962), p. 16.

83 Kubler, *Shape of Time*, p. 17.

84 Henri Focillon, *The Life of Forms in Art*, translated by Charles B. Hogan and George Kubler (New York: Zone, 1989), pp. 44 and 110. First French edition in 1934; first English edition in 1942.

85 Walter Cahn, "L'Art Français et l'Art Allemand," in *Relire Focillon. Cycle de conférences organisé au Musée du Louvre sous la direction de Matthias Waschek* (Paris: Ecole Nationale Supérieure des Beaux-Arts, 1998), p. 36. In 1936 Focillon said of himself: "...je n'ai pas commencé par un système. C'est après avoir longtemps travaillé que j'ai cru pouvoir rédiger quelques conclusions.

Les formes sont l'essentiel, elles combinent entre elles certains rapports, elles dessinent, à travers l'histoire, des parcours que n'explique pas la pure succession des temps, et, plus que la valeur précaire et mobile de leur contenu, elles révèlent la présence éternelle de l'homme. J'ai souhaité d'abord être le naturaliste de ces mondes imaginaires. Et puis il m'a paru plus utile, et peut-être plus beau, de dessiner, même en traits imparfaits, la logique toute particulière qui semble présider à leur création et s'imposer à leur analyse. J'ai tenté d'esquisser le rapport de cette logique et de la vie historique. Mais ce traité de l'enchaînement des effets et des causes reste un traité de la liberté. L'homme n'est pas un produit passif. Il travaille perpétuellement sur lui-même. Il cherche sans répit sa forme et son style." Quoted by Kubler, "Henri Focillon, 1881–1943," *College Art Journal*, IV, no. 2 (1945), reprinted in Kubler's *Studies in Ancient American and European Art: the Collected Essays of George Kubler*, edited by Thomas F. Reese (New Haven: Yale University Press, 1985), pp. 379–380.

86 The Valéry-Focillon proposal put forward in July 1930 is given in full in the November 1931 number of the *Bulletin de La Coopération Intellectuelle*, nos. 7–8 (supplément), citation quoted here, p. 13.

87 Ibid., p. 41.

88 Kubler, *Shape of Time*, pp. 17–18.

89 Henri Focillon, discussion in the session "*Le Lecteur—Besoins et Goûts Nouveaux du Public*," *Entretiens. Le Destin Prochain des Lettres* (Paris: Institut International de Coopération Intellectuelle, 1938), p. 148. The meeting was held July 20–24, 1937 in Paris.

90 "Focillon to Deliver Four Art Lectures," *Yale Daily News*, 7 October, 1937.

91 Announced in the *Yale Daily News* November 1, 2, 9, 16 and 23, 1939.

92 Manuscript copy for the "Plan d'organisation du Département d'Histoire de l'Art, dated January 17, 1940, in the Department of the History of Art Records, Sterling Memorial Library, Manuscripts and Archives Collections, Yale University, RU796, box 1, folder 5.

93 Kubler was joined by the young medievalist Sumner Crosby, the Renaissance specialist Charles Seymour, the Americanist John Baur and the modernist George Heard Hamilton. Kubler has written about these lectures in "The Teaching of Henri Focillon," unpublished paper delivered at Yale University, March 17, 1981 and published in *Studies in Ancient American and European Art*, pp. 384–385. On June 3, 1945, Kubler wrote to Meyer Schapiro, asking him for support for the idea of stretching the scope of reviews in the *Art Bulletin* to include pertinent reading from other disciplines, "such as history, psychology, anthropology and from the exact sciences." Meyer Schapiro Collection, Rare Book and Manuscript Library, Columbia University, MS#1121, series II, box 141, f. 16. Together and separately Focillon's students would take the starting points he gave them in different directions that did not repeat. Baur would go on to direct the Whitney Museum. Hamilton would stay at Yale and make his mark on the study of modern painting with two books published in 1954—one resurrected and mapped the criticism Manet's paintings initially received and the other charted the history of art and architecture in Russia prior to the revolution. But Hamilton's contribution to modern art history is to be gauged as much, if not more, by the passage of Katherine Dreier's Société Anonyme Collection into the Yale Art Gallery in 1941 and by his enthusiasm in the late fifties for translating, at first unasked, Marcel Duchamp's notes for the *Large Glass* into English. George Heard Hamilton, *Manet and his Critics* (New Haven: Yale University Press, 1954) and *The Art and Architecture of Russia*, Pelican History of Art v. 6 (Baltimore: Penguin Books, 1954). Duchamp had published a box of facsimiles of his notes for the *Large Glass* in *La Mariée Mise à Nu par ses Célibataires, Même* (Paris: Rrose Sélavy, 1934). Hamilton's

translations began with *From the Green Box*, 25 notes translated by George Heard Hamilton (New Haven: Readymade Press, 1957) and then when the complete group was published in French by Michel Sanouillet in 1959 as *Marchand du Sel. Ecrits de Marcel Duchamp* (Paris: Terrain Vague, 1959), he undertook the rest in collaboration with Richard Hamilton, *The Bride Stripped Bare by Her Bachelors, Even*, typographic design by Richard Hamilton, translated by George Heard Hamilton (New York: Wittenborn, 1960). George Hamilton would also rescue the English translation of Robert Lebel's *Sur Marcel Duchamp* (New York: Trianon, 1959), a complicated matter: see Paul B. Franklin, "1959: Headline, Duchamp," *Etant donné Marcel Duchamp*, no. 7 (2006), pp. 141–175.

94 All that remains of this turn in his thinking are a few asides in his late work and the notes taken down by his students. The asides can be found in Focillon's last book, *Moyen Age. Survivances et Réveils. Etudes d'Art et d'Histoire* (New York: Brentano's, 1943), p. 11 with its opposition to Hegelian becoming: "pour nous, l'histoire est plutôt comme un empilage de couches géologiques dont certaines failles brusques, certains <<canyons>> font apparaître d'un seul coup aux yeux du voyageur la simultanéité dans la durée." For its asides see, for example, George Kubler's notes and the photocopies he made of Sumner Crosby's notes, both to be found in the George Alexander Kubler Papers, Sterling Memorial Library, Yale University Library, Manuscripts and Archives, 1997–M–022, box 10. They each took down slightly different versions of these lectures, as one might expect. Focillon was building on the work of others and in terms of the sociological questions, it is important to cite Jean-Marie Guyau, *L'Art au point de vue sociologique* (Paris: Belin, 1887).

95 Focillon, *Life of Forms in Art*, p. 156.

96 The course was titled "L'histoire de l'art et la vie de l'esprit," and the notes for these lectures, dated Washington, 1941 (Focillon was in residence at Dumbarton Oaks), are published in *Relire Focillon*, pp. 171–183, the citation here from p. 183. According to Kubler's

notes, Focillon appears only to have given one lecture on method, and it concerned medieval architecture, to the students at Yale that winter.

97 Focillon, "A Nos Amis d'Argentine," *Témoignage pour la France* (New York: Brentano's, 1945), pp. 40–41.

98 Again, these lectures were given in French, with French titles: "Quarante-huit. Une époque, un art"; "Romantisme et réalisme. Courbet"; "L'homme des champs. Millet"; "La Caricature épique. Daumier" on October 20, 22, 29 and November 5, 1940 respectively. The *Yale Daily News* announced them one by one and on October 29 interviewed Focillon, "Focillon to Discuss French Art Today."

99 Focillon, intervention in *Entretiens. L'Art et la Réalité. L'Art et l'Etat* (Paris: Institut International de Coopération Intellectuelle, 1934), p. 62.

100 Focillon, "Fonction Universelle de la France," *Témoignage*, pp. 52, 58, 61–63.

101 Kubler, *Shape of Time*, p. 18.

102 Focillon, "L'Ecole Libre des Hautes-Etudes de New-York," *Témoignage*, pp. 113–117.

103 Aristide R. Zolberg, "The Ecole Libre at the New School 1941–1946," *Social Research*, v. 65 (December 1998), pp. 921–951.

104 Focillon, "La Démocratie et la Vague du Passé," *Témoignage*, p. 190.

105 Focillon, *The Year 1000*, translated by Fred D. Wieck (New York: Frederick Ungar, 1969), pp. 22–23.

106 Kubler, *Shape of Time*, pp. 17–19. The notebook containing the first handwritten draft with a receipt from Yale University Press dated November 1960 is now found in the George Alexander Kubler Papers,

Sterling Memorial Library, Yale University Library, Manuscripts and Archives, 1997–M–022, box 4.

107 *Shape of Time*, p. 20.

108 Ibid., p. 61.

109 Ibid., p. 125.

110 Robert Horvitz, "A Talk with George Kubler," *Artforum* (October 1973), p. 32.

111 Ibid., p. 34.

112 See the notice written by Christiane Moatti for *Les Voix du Silence*, in André Malraux, *Ecrits sur l'art*, t. I (Paris: Pléiade, 2004), p. 1334.

113 Leo Steinberg, "Other Criteria," first given as a lecture at MoMA in March 1968 and reprinted in his book by the same title, *Other Criteria: Confrontations with Twentieth-Century Art* (New York: Oxford University Press, 1972), pp. 55–91. Lucy Lippard, *Six Years: the Dematerialization of the Art Object from 1966 to 1972* (New York: Praeger, 1973).

114 Meyer Schapiro, "Nature of Abstract Art," op. cit., and "Courbet and Popular Imagery: an Essay in Realism and Naiveté," *Journal of the Warburg and Courtauld Institutes*, v. 4 (1940–41), pp. 164–191. Schapiro sent one of his 10 offprints to Focillon. See the undated letter from Focillon's wife Marguerite thanking Schapiro for the Courbet offprint, Meyer Schapiro Collection, Rare Book and Manuscript Library, Columbia University, MS#1121, series II, box 127, folder 3.

115 Schapiro, "Courbet and Popular Imagery," op. cit., p. 173. The citation comes from Pierre Dupont's "Les Deux Compagnons du Devoir," from his *Muse Populaire*.

116 Ibid., p. 185 for Marx and for Baudelaire, p. 180.

117 Robert L. Herbert, "City vs. Country: the Rural Image in French Painting from Millet to Gauguin," *Artforum* (February 1970), pp. 44–55; reprinted, with many fewer illustrations, in his book, *From Millet to Léger: Essays in Social Art History* (New Haven: Yale University Press, 2002), pp. 23–48. The preface to the book describes his relation to Schapiro and to Hamilton, pp. vi–xi. See also his catalogue essay in *Seurat and the Making of La Grande Jatte* (Chicago: The Art Institute of Chicago, 2004), pp. 158–160. Herbert began a correspondence with Schapiro in 1953, now in the Meyer Schapiro Collection, Rare Book and Manuscript Library, Columbia University, MS#1121, series II, box 133, f. 10.

118 Weiner's work illustrated the article by Jack Burnham, "Alice's Head: Reflections on Conceptual Art," *Artforum* (February 1970), p. 41. See Christian Rattemeyer, "*Op Losse Schroeven*: Tentative Connections," in Christophe Chérix, *In and Out of Amsterdam: Travels in Conceptual Art, 1960–1976* (New York: MoMA, 2009), pp. 37–44. Technical information on the flare provided by Weiner in correspondence with the author, May 7, 2011.

119 Meyer Schapiro, typed letter to Henri Focillon, dated May 9, 1936, quoted by Walter Cahn, "Schapiro and Focillon," *Gesta*, v. 41 (2002), p. 134. In the same letter, Schapiro distinguishes his view of sociological material from that of Taine: "I am not a disciple of Taine; if there is any social thinker whose views guide me, I would say that he is Karl Marx, rather than Taine; and there is all the difference in the world between their conceptions of society and the driving forces of history. Taine presents us the various arts as reflections or expressions of given societies and environments (or races); but he cannot explain why society changes; he lacks an historical dynamic. He is a positivist with certain romantic notions of culture as an expression of social individuality, but he is not an historical materialist. I am aware of certain difficulties in the theory of historical materialism, but I do not consider

them inherent in the theory; they belong rather to certain narrow and mechanical formulations. I accept it as an hypothesis for approaching history and society, in which art is one element."

120 Herbert, "City vs. Country," op. cit., p. 53.

121 Ibid., p. 55.

122 Robert L. Herbert and Eugenia W. Herbert, "Artists and Anarchism: Unpublished Letters of Pissarro, Signac and Others—I," *The Burlington Magazine,* v. 102 (November 1960), p. 481.

123 Ibid., p. 482. The second part of the article appears in the December issue of the *Burlington,* pp. 517–522. These articles followed from Robert Herbert's work on Seurat, published initially as "Seurat's Drawings," in *Seurat: Paintings and Drawings,* edited by Daniel Catton Rich (Chicago: The Art Institute and New York: MoMA, 1958), and "Seurat in Chicago and New York," *The Burlington Magazine,* v. 100 (May 1958), pp. 146–155, and from Eugenia W. Herbert's thesis, published as *The Artist and Social Reform: France and Belgium 1885–1898* (New Haven: Yale University Press, 1961). His work appeared as *Seurat's Drawings* (New York: Dover, 1963). At this time Herbert would begin his work on the Barbizon school and on modern art theory, editing the *The Art Criticism of John Ruskin* (New York: Da Capo, 1964) and *Modern Artists on Art* (Englewood Cliffs: Prentice Hall, 1964).

124 Herbert, "City vs. Country," op. cit., p. 55.

125 See especially: E. P. Thompson, *The Making of the English Working Class* (London: Victor Gollancz, 1963). Raymond Williams' two books, *Culture and Society* (London: Chatto and Windus, 1958) and *The Long Revolution* (London: Chatto and Windus, 1961). Arnold Hauser, *Sozialgeschichte der Kunst und Literatur,* 2 vols. (Munich: C. H. Beck, 1953), with an English edition first, *The Social History of Art* (New York: Alfred A. Knopf, 1951); and then

his *Philosophie der Kunstgeschichte* (Munich: C. H. Beck, 1958), with an English edition following, *The Philosophy of Art History* (New York: Alfred A. Knopf, 1959).

126 T. J. Clark, "A Bourgeois Dance of Death: Max Buchon on Courbet," *The Burlington Magazine*, v. 111 (April 1969), pp. 208–213 and (May 1969), pp. 286–290.

127 T. J. Clark, *Image of the People: Gustave Courbet and the 1848 Revolution* (London: Thames & Hudson, 1973), pp. 9–20. The book was issued in tandem with *The Absolute Bourgeois: Artists and Politics in France, 1848–1851* (London: Thames & Hudson, 1973).

128 Ibid., p. 78.

129 See Clark's contribution, "Preliminary Arguments: Work of Art and Ideology," to the Marxism and Art History Session of the College Art Association Meeting in Chicago, February 1976 (mimeograph, 1977), lamenting the banalities into which the word "experience" had fallen. "`After experience, ideology?`" he wrote, adding presciently, "`Perhaps-but even that, remember, is a concept which could be recuperated, on its own.`"

130 Ibid., p. 18.

131 See Smithson's account, "Entropy Made Visible" an interview with Alison Sky in 1973, published in *On Site #4* (1973), reprinted in *The Writings of Robert Smithson*, edited by Nancy Holt (New York: New York University Press, 1979), pp. 194–196. The best historical account is to be found in Ann Reynolds, *Robert Smithson: Learning from New Jersey and Elsewhere* (Cambridge: MIT Press, 2003).

132 For a good range of case histories detailing both the Old and the New Left's contribution to art history, see *Marxism and the History of Art: from William Morris to the New Left*, edited by Andrew Hemingway (London: Pluto Press, 2006). For Linda Nochlin, see her essay "Why Are There No Great Women Artists?" in *Women in*

Sexist Society, edited by Vivian Gornick and Barbara Moran (New York: Basic Books, 1971), pp. 344–366, and reprinted, illustrated and edited, as "Why Have There Been No Great Women Artists?" *ARTnews* (January 1971), pp. 22–39, 67–71; and her earlier articles, "Gustave Courbet's Meeting: A Portrait of the Artist as a Wandering Jew" *The Art Bulletin*, Vol. 49, No. 3 (September 1967), pp. 209–222, and "The Invention of the Avant-Garde," *Art News Annual*, v. XXXIV (1968), reprinted in *Avant-Garde Art*, edited by Thomas B. Hess and John Ashbery (New York: Macmillan, 1968), pp. 1–24. These laid the ground for her book, *Realism* (Harmondsworth: Penguin, 1971).

133 *The Misc* (April 3, 1970) announces a lecture by Nochlin (she had married Richard Pommer in 1968): "The Image of Women in 19th and 20th Century Art" in Taylor Hall: "Mrs. Pommer's lecture is the outcome of research for her seminar, "Problems in Twentieth Century Art." She is also preparing a lecture on an aspect of this topic at NYU and an anthology of women's liberation articles."

134 André Malraux, *Les Voix du Silence* (Paris: NRF, 1951), p. 276.

135 Linda Nochlin, "Why Have There Been No Great Women Artists?" *ARTnews* (January 1971), p. 25.

136 See Lucy Lippard's account of the exhibition in Hans Ulrich Obrist, *A Brief History of Curating* (Zurich: JPR/Ringier, 2008), pp. 224–225.

137 Gordon Matta-Clark's telegram to Vassar, reproduced in the catalogue for *26 x 26* (Vassar College Art Gallery, Poughkeepsie, New York, May 1–June 6, 1971). He made what he called a "Celestial Drawing" of the tree, now in the collection of Vassar's Frances Lehman Loeb Art Center. On the back of the drawing he noted: "I think of the tree climb as an aerial dance during which I overcome the discomfort of empty space by installing a resting place in which my body will be supported while

aloft." A film was made that summer showing different moments of the *Tree Dance: Tree Dance*, 1971, 9:32 minutes, 16 mm film.

138 Carol Goodden letter to the author, December 9, 2007.

139 Nochlin, "Why Have There Been No Great Women Artists?" op. cit., p. 70.

140 Hannah Arendt, "Thinking and Moral Considerations," in *Responsibility and Judgment*, edited by Jerome Kohn (New York: Schocken, 2003), p. 178.

141 Ibid., pp. 188–189.

142 Grace Glueck, "U.S. Decides Not to Take Part In São Paolo Bienal This Year," *New York Times*, May 31, 1971. On the larger context for the protest, see Luis Camnitzer, "The Museo Latinoameriano and MICLA," in *A Principality of Its Own: 40 Years of Visual Arts at the Americas Society*, edited by José Luis Falconi and Gabriela Rangel (New York: Harvard University Press, 2006), pp. 216–229.

Illustrations

Harper & Brothers, 1924) p. 481. Picasso's painting, oil on canvas, 58 × 37.4 in (147 × 95 cm), belongs to the State Pushkin Museum of Fine Arts, Moscow. © 2019 Estate of Pablo Picasso / Artists Rights Society (ARS), New York.

p. 34 Vincent Van Gogh, *Crows in a Wheatfield*, 1890. Oil on canvas, 19.9 × 48.6 in (69. 6 × 122. 6 cm). Van Gogh Museum, Amsterdam (The Vincent Van Gogh Foundation).

p. 35 Isamu Noguchi, Cover, *View*, series VI, no. 5 (October 1946). Courtesy of Indra B. Tamang. © 2020 The Isamu Noguchi Foundation and Garden Museum, New York / Artists Rights Society (ARS), New York.

p. 37 Francis Lee, Picasso in his Studio, *View*, series VI, nos. 2–3 (March–April 1946) p. 16.

p. 38 Jackson Pollock, *Eyes in the Heat*, 1946. Oil and enamel on canvas, 54 × 43 in (137.2 × 109.2 cm). Solomon R. Guggenheim Foundation, Peggy Guggenheim Collection, Venice. © 2019 The Pollock-Krasner Foundation / Artists Rights Society (ARS), New York.

p. 42 Alexander Dorner, Diagram of the Dissolution of the Western Picture of Three-Dimensional Reality, *The Way Beyond 'Art'—the Work of Herbert Bayer* (New York: Wittenborn, 1947) p. 229. Courtesy Wittenborn Art Books, San Francisco.

p. 44 El Lissitzky, *Abstract Cabinet*, 1925 (now destroyed), commissioned as a period room, Hannover Landesmuseum, as illustrated in Dorner, *The Way Beyond 'Art'—the Work of Herbert Bayer* (New York: Wittenborn, 1947) p. 115. © 2013 Artists Rights Society (ARS), New York. Courtesy Wittenborn Art Books, San Francisco

p. 46 Alfred Barr Jr., Diagram of Whistler's Composition, *What is Modern Painting?* (New York: The Museum of Modern Art,

1943) p. 12. Digital Image © The Museum of Modern Art/Licensed by SCALA / Art Resource, NY.

p. 47 Frank Stella, *The Marriage of Reason and Squalor, II,* 1959. Enamel on canvas, 90.75 × 132.75 in (230.5 × 337.2 cm). Larry Aldrich Foundation Fund. The Museum of Modern Art, New York / Licensed by SCALA / Art Resources, NY. © 2019 Frank Stella / Artists Rights Society (ARS), New York.

p. 48 Advertisement, National Dairy Products Corporation, Marshall McLuhan, *The Mechanical Bride: Folklore of Industrial Man* (New York: Vanguard, 1951) p. 142. Courtesy of Gingko Press.

p. 49 Robert Capa, "Loyalist Militiaman at the Moment of Death, Cerro Muriano, September 5, 1936," *LIFE* (July 12, 1937) pp. 18–19. © 1937 The Picture Collection Inc. All rights reserved. Reprinted/ Translated from *LIFE* and published with permission of The Picture Collection Inc. Reproduction in any manner in any language in whole or in part without written permission is prohibited.

p. 51 Cover, *Information,* ed. Kynaston McShine (New York: The Museum of Modern Art, 1970). Digital Image © The Museum of Modern Art/Licensed by SCALA / Art Resource, NY.

p. 52 Robert Smithson, *Spiral Jetty,* Rozelle Point, Great Salt Lake, Utah, April 1970. Mud, precipitated salt crystals, rocks, water coil, 1500' long and 15' wide. Collection: Dia Center for the Arts, New York. Photo: Gianfranco Gorgoni. © Holt/Smithson Foundation and Dia Art Foundation / VAGA at Artists Rights Society (ARS), NY.

p. 53 Art Workers' Coalition (Frazier Dougherty, Jon Hendricks, Irving Petlin), "Q: And babies?" 1970, lithograph. The Museum of Modern Art, New York. Digital Image © The Museum of Modern Art/Licensed by SCALA / Art Resource, NY.

p. 61 George Kubler, Notecard Summing up Focillon's Lectures. Circa 1940, inscribed later in Kubler's hand, paper card,

5 × 8 in (12.7 × 20.32 cm). George Alexander Kubler Papers, 1872–2000 (inclusive). Sterling Memorial Library, Manuscripts and Archives Collections, Yale University.

p. 70 Lawrence Weiner, *THE RESIDUE OF A FLARE IGNITED UPON A BOUNDARY*, 1969. Language and materials, dimensions variable. Solomon R. Guggenheim Museum, New York, Panza Collection, Gift 92.4180. © 2019 Lawrence Weiner / Artists Rights Society (ARS), New York.

p. 73 J.-F. Millet, *The Sower*, 1850. Oil on canvas, 40 × 32.5 in (101.6 × 82.6 cm) Museum of Fine Arts, Boston. Photograph © 2020 Museum of Fine Arts, Boston.

p. 75 Robert L. Herbert, "City vs. Country: The Rural Image in French Painting from Millet to Gauguin," *Artforum* (February 1970), p. 54. © Artforum, February 1970, "City vs. Country: The Rural Image in French Painting from Millet to Gauguin," by Robert L. Herbert, p.54.

p. 77 Gustave Courbet, *A Burial at Ornans*, 1849–1850. Oil on canvas, 124 × 260 in (315 × 668 cm). Musée d'Orsay, Paris. © RMN-Grand Palais / Art Resource, NY.

p. 81 Cover, *ARTnews* (January 1971). Copyright © Art Media, LLC ARTnews, LLC, January, 2020.

p. 83 Gordon Matta-Clark, Telegram to Mary Delahoyd, Curator at the Vassar College Art Gallery, for Use as his Artist's Statement in the Catalogue for the Exhibition, *26 × 26*, at Vassar College, 1971. Centre Canadien d'Architecture / Canadian Centre for Architecture, Montreal. Canadian Centre for Architecture. Gift of Estate of Gordon Matta-Clark.

p. 85, 87, 89 Gordon Matta-Clark, Stills from *Tree Dance*, 1971. © 2019 Estate of Gordon Matta-Clark / Artists Rights Society (ARS), New York.

Index

Acknowledgments

This volume introduces a series, *Pre-Occupations*, designed to collect the essays, old and new, written alongside my other projects. The first of these essays appeared during the work on *Atget's Seven Albums*, finished in 1989, and *Their Common Sense*, finished in 1996. Afterwards they came in combination with *Utopia Station*, which began as a collective book project in the summer of 2001 and shortly thereafter, in 2002, became a large ongoing exhibition experiment with Hans Ulrich Obrist and Rirkrit Tiravanija. At every step the essay collection has been collective, more broadly speaking: there have been rich and real exchanges with many fellow travelers, writers, artists, students, and friends too numerous to name; every one remains for me a spark. *The Pragmatism in the History of Art* has allowed me to reflect on a process that has been a lifelong search for better illumination.

No one works in isolation, least of all those prospecting on history's cliffs. For this volume I would like to especially thank the librarians and archivists at Beinecke Library and Sterling Memorial Library's Manuscripts and Archives Collections at Yale University, the Rare Book and Manuscript Library at Columbia University, the Museum of Modern Art Archives in New York, and the Canadian Centre for Architecture Archives in Montreal. I would also like to formally thank Jean Baltrušaitis, Jane Crawford, Carol Goodden McCoy, Chris Marker, Richard Nonas, and Lawrence Weiner here for their confidence, precision, and counsel. Chelsea Weathers and Jenn Shapland have organized the image permissions; Angela Brown has provided editorial assistance. Gloria Kury expertly shepherded the first edition to publication at Periscope Publishing in 2013. Adam Michaels created the perceptive and intellectually sensitive design that now defines the *Pre-Occupations* series. He and Shannon Harvey have subsequently taken on the publication of the series at Inventory Press. I remain deeply grateful to all for their solidarity and support.

The Creative Capital / Andy Warhol Foundation Arts Writers Grant Program gave me the opportunity to conceive this series of volumes. *The Pragmatism in the History of Art* has been made possible by the Foundation's Program as well as by The Anne McNiff Tatlock '61 Endowment for Strategic Faculty Support and The Lucy Maynard Salmon Research Fund of Vassar College. Additional support for the second printing has been provided by The Irving and Marilyn Lavin Fund of the Institute for Advanced Study, Princeton.

Some of the thoughts contained in the present volume developed in preparation for the J. Kirk T. Varnedoe Memorial Lectures at the Institute of Fine Arts, New York University in the spring of 2008. Some were sketched for "Light in Buffalo" in *Thinking Worlds: The Moscow Conference on Philosophy, Politics and Art,* edited by Joseph Backstein, Daniel Birbaum, and Sven-Olov Wallenstein (Berlin: Sternberg Press, 2008), pp. 105–121, reprinted in the catalogue for the 2009 Venice Biennale, *Making Worlds: 53rd International Exhibition,* directed by Daniel Birnbaum (Venice: Marsilio, 2009), v.1, pp. 225-231.

About the Author

Molly Nesbit is the Mary Conover Mellon Chair of Art History at Vassar College and a contributing editor of *Artforum*. Her books include Atget's *Seven Albums* (Yale University Press, 1992) and *Their Common Sense* (Black Dog, 2000). Since 2002, together with Hans Ulrich Obrist and Rirkrit Tiravanija, she has been curating the succession of *Utopia Stations*, an ongoing collective book, exhibition, seminar, web and street project. *The Pragmatism in the History of Art* (Periscope, 2013), is the first volume of *Pre-Occupations*, a series collecting her essays; the second, *Midnight: The Tempest Essays*, was published in 2017 by Inventory Press.

The Pragmatism in the History of Art
is published by
Inventory Press, LLC
2305 Hyperion Ave.
Los Angeles, CA 90027
inventorypress.com

Design: IN-FO.CO

Printed and bound in Singapore
by Pristone

ISBN: 978-1-941753-27-9
LCCN: 2019955255

Distributed by
ARTBOOK | D.A.P.
75 Broad Street, Suite 630
New York, NY 10004
artbook.com

Publication of this book was aided by the Creative Capital/Andy Warhol Foundation Arts Writers Grant Program.

Arts
Writers
Grant
Program

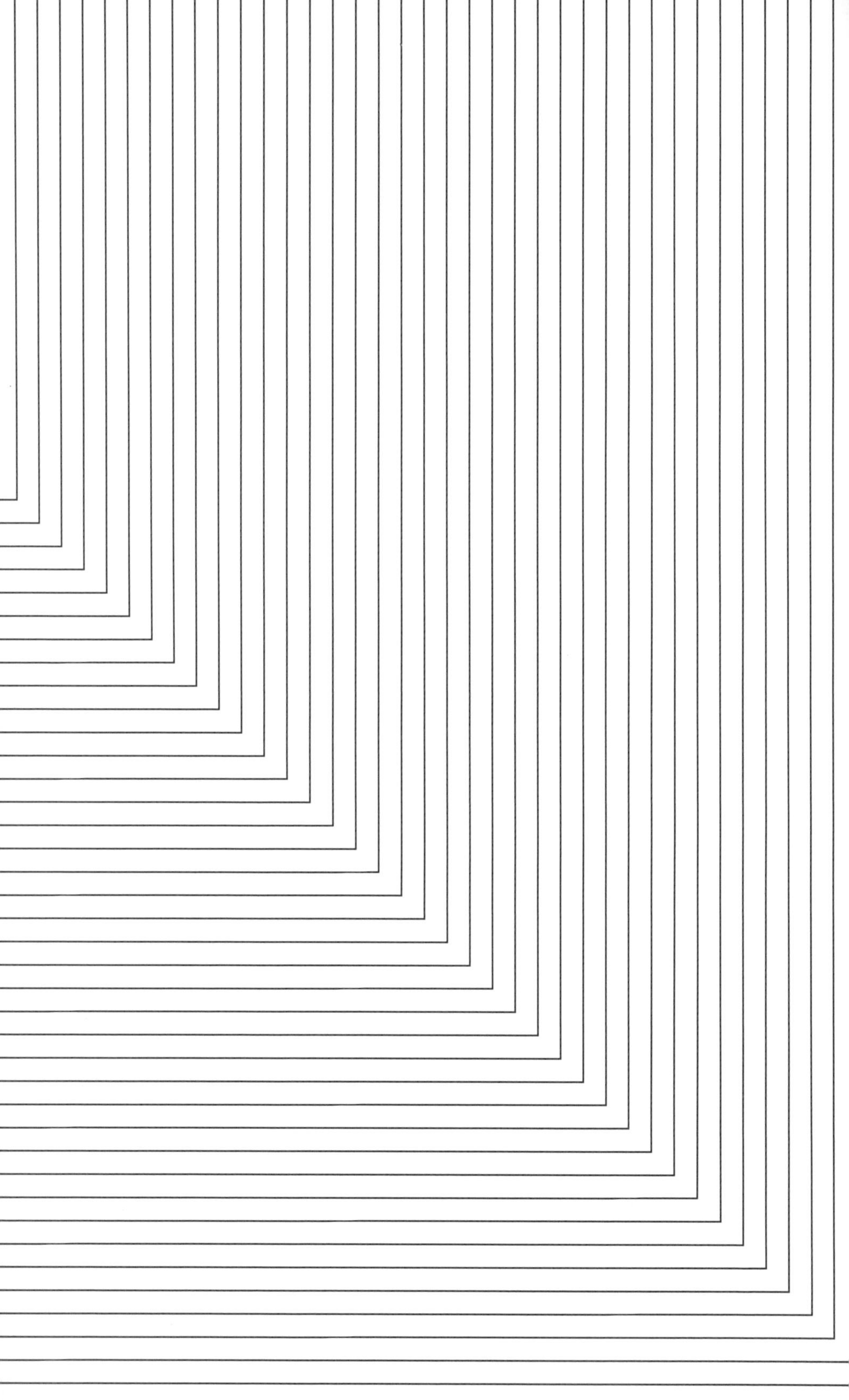